BROKEN BODY, WOUNDED SPIRIT:

BALANCING THE SEE-SAW OF CHRONIC PAIN

WINTER DEVOTIONS

(Revised, 2014)

Thank you for taking
the journey with me.
In healing,
Celeste

CelesteCooper.com

WINTER DEVOTIONS

Inside the Cover

"This lovely book of devotions is rich with insight and practical suggestions for any one with chronic pain. It is filled with inspirational and healing words dealing with topics from nutrition, exercise, and sleep to relating successfully to your doctor."

Susan E. Opper, MD, Medical Director of Saint Luke's Pain Management Services, Saint Luke's Hospital of Kansas City.

"I love the very idea of 'Winter Devotions'. The struggle of living with chronic pain is compounded for many by the winter months when it is cold, damp, and often gloomy. Bones ache, joints hurts, and the spirit sometimes become depressed. This wonderful book provides a tool to help with those issues. The quotes, photography, and motivation of authors Celeste Cooper and Jeff Miller all bring much needed hope and relief."

Myra J. Christopher, Kathleen M. Foley Chair in Pain and Palliative Care at the Center for Practical Bioethics practicalbioethics.org/, and Principal Investigator of the Pain Action Alliance to Implement a National Strategy, PAINSproject.org/.

"Chronic pain is a tyrant that seeks to control every aspect of a person's life—body, mind, and spirit. Broken Body, Wounded Spirit offers pain sufferers' guidance in fending off the tyrant and regaining control over their lives. Celeste and Jeff do a beautiful job of blending practical suggestions, inspirational quotes, and delightful seasonal images into daily nuggets of wisdom that uplift and fortify the body, mind, and spirit."

Karen Lee Richards, Fibromyalgia Editor, ProHealth, prohealth.com/, and Chronic Pain Health Guide, HealthCentral, healthcentral.com/chronic-pain/.

"Broken Body, Wounded Spirit is a warm and thoughtful prescription to honor oneself in the face of challenge, not just chronic pain. It is perfectly sprinkled with invaluable wisdom to address every aspect of wellbeing. This is a laugh out loud toolkit with humorous sayings, photos and lessons for lifestyle change bundled into a special 90-day guide to celebrate health."

Lisa Marianni, RN, MBA, Consultant and previous Senior Director, Sharecare Provider Solutions in Atlanta, GA

"Dealing with chronic pain can make us feel robbed of many choices. We can succumb to 'woe is me' or we can work on self-management skills. This book offers tips and tools which can be utilized to enable us to 'participate in life' rather than 'watch it go by' from the sidelines. What will you choose?"

Orvie Prewitt, Program Coordinator – Kansas City Regional Arthritis Center, and a person living with chronic pain.

"As welcome as a spring breeze, this inspiring book series gently encourages fresh perspectives for living well with chronic pain or illness. Whether pondering one day at a time or dancing between the pages, the insightful prose leads the reader to feelings of peaceful dignity. A unique celebration of living harmoniously with the seasons of the year while rejuvenating ourselves physically and spiritually. Thanks Celeste for sharing your sparkling love for life!"

Jan Favero Chambers, President/Founder of the National Fibromyalgia & Chronic Pain Association, fmcpaware.org. *"Your partner in tackling fibromyalgia and chronic pain."*

"Anyone with chronic pain can and will be helped by reading and using this book as a tool. It is the perfect blend of inspiration and helpful information to guide people on their pain journey, in fact, as a person with pain; I have learned some important techniques that have helped me."

Paul Gileno, Founder/President, US Pain Foundation Inc. uspainfoundation.org.

....

BROKEN BODY, WOUNDED SPIRIT:
Balancing the See-Saw of Chronic Pain

....

WINTER DEVOTIONS

Celeste Cooper, RN, BSN

and

Jeff Miller, PhD

Missouri

FOREWORD

"The Broken Body, Wounded Spirit: Balancing the See-Saw of Chronic Pain" series offers an integrative holistic approach to chronic pain conditions and is what is needed in medicine today. Empowering us to become part of our own health and healing process is such a powerful approach to these conditions or any others. I applaud the authors, and hope they inspire others to follow their lead. The inspirational healing words and information on nutrition and exercise and the importance of quality sleep are a treasure trove for anyone dealing with chronic pain conditions."

Bill Douglas, author of the best–selling tai chi book, "***The Complete Idiot's Guide to T'ai Chi & Qigong***," and Founder of World Tai Chi & Qigong Day and World Healing Day. Bill teaches Tai Chi for people with chronic pain conditions through the University of Kansas Hospital's Turning Point program.

ACKNOWLEDGMENTS

The authors began this journey well over decade ago. To know that so many people support what we are doing with this book series, even though they do not have chronic pain themselves, gives us hope for changing the way pain is perceived, judged, and treated.

Writing with inspiration provides personal fulfillment, and we could not have done it without the steadfast support of our colleagues, friends, and family, but most of all, our readers. Those who follow our work are generous with their feedback, and they continue to let us know that the experiences we share are important in their lives.

We understand that chronic pain can deprive a person of their dignity, and we cannot stress enough that you, our readers, and fellow patients are important to us. This series is a tribute to all of the observant people before us and with us who were, and are, committed to helping the chronic pain person be their best self.

"If we had no winter, the spring would not be so pleasant:
if we did not sometimes taste of adversity,
prosperity would not be so welcome."

~ Anne Bradstreet, from The Works of Anne Bradstreet

ॐ

And we're off. There was a time when any notes in the margins of schoolbooks came with a penalty. I wonder now, was there an eraser posse that thumbed through every page of every textbook I ever returned?

We have created a series of books for *Broken Body, Wounded Spirit: Balancing the See-Saw of Chronic Pain* that encourages our readers to interact with the material. Feel the freedom of writing wherever you want to write, we encourage it, because this is your book to use as your own personal reference for your progress.

In an effort to avoid too many blank pages, maintain format, yet give extra space for notes, we have dispersed pages throughout the book for you to write your thoughts, hopes, and desires. You can locate extra NOTE pages in the index so you can fast-forward to the next NOTE page from your location. Take a moment to dog-ear the index page for your reference.

Best wishes on your journey.

ॐ

INTRODUCTION

The winter season is often compared to death. In this case, it is the dying off of old thoughts and destructive behaviors. Because of this, we must experience many feelings, good and bad, so we can be born into a new way of thinking about chronic pain and how it affects us all.

When pain is in "boss mode," it detracts from our innate need to socialize and contribute. Confronting chronic pain takes constant reminders. We need motivation to conquer our fears just as sales people need motivation to stay focused on their goals and achievements. *"Winter Devotions"* promotes the motivation necessary for dealing with the effects pain can impose on our lives physically, mentally, emotionally, and spiritually, and it provides the tools we need for setting healthy goals.

Each book in this series offers different perspectives for conquering obstacles and improving personal beliefs. The daily devotions act as the catalyst we need in healing our perceptions.

Come with us as we walk the barren winter land, appreciating the necessity to rid ourselves of previous perceptions and prepare for the spring season of rebirth.

"Eventually one gets to the Medicine Wheel
to fulfill one's life."

~ Old Mouse, elder
of the Arikara tribe of North Dakota

❧ *W*inter ❧
Day One

The Power of the Circle

"You have noticed that everything an Indian does is in a circle, and that is because the Power of the World always works in circles, and everything tries to be round... The Sky is round, and I have heard that the earth is round like a ball and so are all the stars. The wind, in its greatest power, whirls. Birds make their nest in circles, for theirs is the same religion as ours..."

~ Black Elk Oglala Sioux Holy Man, 1863-1950

The value of this perception has been recognized for many centuries. The "Native American Medicine Wheel" is a reflection of the strengths and weaknesses from which we all draw wisdom, and it is influenced by our physical, mental, emotional, and spiritual self, an inherent belief of great religions.

Working towards total balance is a lofty goal, one we may not ever fully achieve, but it is important to see the lesson as we make the journey. When we are mired down in physical pain, we can lighten the load by focusing on exercises for building our mental, emotional, and spiritual awareness during this season of rest and rejuvenation.

How can I find balance in my strengths and weakness?

Life happens.
Fix what you can and accept the rest.

~ Celeste

❧ *Winter* ❧
Day Two

Wake Up Sleepy Head: Are You Deprived?

"Melatonin is a brain chemical produced when the brain receives a signal from the eye that daylight is ending. In contrast, when your brain perceives the light impulse, melatonin production shuts down and allows you to awaken. This is why it is important to maintain regular sleep habits."

(Excerpt, *Integrative Therapies for Fibromyalgia, Chronic Fatigue Syndrome, and Myofascial Pain*... Cooper and Miller, Healing Arts Press, 2010.)

If we take advantage of the early and expanded hours of darkness during winter, the season of rest, it provides us the opportunity to practice good sleep hygiene. This is important because sleep deprivation affects our mental, physical, emotional, and spiritual health. It weakens the immune response and leaves us more susceptible to other diseases and disorders.

- Avoid over stimulation near bedtime: exercise, over eating, alcohol, nicotine, and medication or foods known to have stimulants.
- Sleep in a comfortable atmosphere and in comfortable attire.

- Deal with stressors requiring resolution during daytime hours.
- Employ relaxation techniques that have worked for you in the past.
- Reduce external stimuli.
- Clear your mind by writing in your journal.
- Read a boring book.
- Keep to a sleep schedule.

I will take advantage of winter darkness to improve my sleep habits.

Notes

ॐ

"What lies behind us and what lies before us are tiny matters compared to what lies within us."

~ Ralph Waldo Emerson, 1803-1882

❧ *W*inter ❧
Day Three

When Our Free Will Is at Risk

Our pain and fatigue are not obvious to those around us. While certain conditions share characteristics and other related symptoms, we are individuals with our own set of unique circumstances and being.

Nevertheless, pain and fatigue are obvious blocks to well–being for all living things. As a result, we encounter feelings of abandonment, absentmindedness, anxiety, anger, insecurity, isolation, low self–confidence, low energy, distrust, conflict, criticism, defensiveness, depression, fear, neediness, mood swings, lack of remorse, negativity, resentment, over sensitivity, and sadness. If allowed to fester, such feelings can block our personal growth and our physical, mental, emotional, and spiritual balance.

While we may not be able to rid ourselves of pain, we can use our free will to find healthy ways of coping. The first step of coping in a healthy way is to identify personal obstacles.

Make it my New Year's resolution to use my free will to identify blocks to growth and balance.

9

My course, navigating the sea of life, begins with a goal
sighted in the lens of my telescope.

~ Celeste

❧ *Winter* ❧
Day Four

Allopathic vs. Naturopathic Medicine

The fact we still exist as a species on earth is not the result of allopathic medicine interventions, a recent concept, but on the body's ability to heal itself if it is cared for properly.

Allopathic medicine serves best the causes and symptoms created by our new industrial, chemical, and synthetic world, i.e. cancer, toxic states, and pandemics. The allopathic medical doctors, such as the MD or DO, diagnose disease and treat it by repressing symptoms or treating the disease. (See more on "Allopathic Medicine" in *Fall Devotions.*)

Naturopathic medicine is based on the concept that health is not the absence of symptoms; it is the absence of cause of the symptoms. In other words, the naturopathic doctor (ND) will treat the patient with the goal of sustaining and strengthening the body's natural resources. Naturopathy is a discipline that promotes a healthy lifestyle through the integration of exercise, stress reduction, and a proper diet consisting of natural, organic foods.

Both, allopathic and naturopathic doctors believe prevention and a healthy lifestyle are important and when the allopathic doctor integrates complimentary alternative medicine, it provides a holistic approach.

11

*"Whatever is true, whatever is honest, whatever is just,
whatever is pure, whatever is lovely, whatever is kind,
if there is any virtue, if there is anything worthy of praise,
think on these things."*

~ Philippians 4:8, NIV

❧ *Winter* ❧
Day Five

Snow Blowing Through Thought Accumulation

As we accumulate thoughts, our brain automatically starts to organize them for future reference. This categorization also holds true for our personal journal, which teaches us about core strengths and understanding of others and self. We should be ready to reorganize our brain's file system with folders containing encouraging thoughts and feelings while cleaning out unnecessary thought accumulation that is accomplished through journaling.

Tips for event journaling:

- Happenings surrounding:
  - A new job.
  - Starting school.
  - A celebration, such as a wedding or birthday.
  - The Birth of a new family member.
- How did the event make you feel?
- Why was the event important to you?
- What was going on around you during the event?
- Who was there?
- Did the event change your life in some way?

How did I clear my path today and take out unnecessary accumulated thoughts with event journaling?

"The purpose of life is a life of purpose."

~ Robert Byrne

❧ *W*inter ❧

Day Six

Are the Runners on Your Sled Worn out?

How did your pain or fatigue affect you yesterday?

Activities of bathing, dressing, eating:

0   2   4   6   8   10

none   completely

Social relationships:

0   2   4   6   8   10

none   completely

Enjoyment of life:

0   2   4   6   8   10

none   completely

What did I do yesterday or the day before that affected this outcome in a positive or negative way?

*Success is measured by behaviors that overcome defeat
and seek the light in the face of obstacles.*

~ Celeste

❧ *Winter* ❧
Day Seven

Recognizing the Value of Illness

Recognizing the value of illness is getting to know oneself, thinking more positively, and achieving a higher awareness of people and things.

We can:

- Find support.
- Make new friends.
- Find new ways of looking at illness.
- Qualify for handicapped parking.
- Embrace alternatives (meditation, visualization, prayer, yoga, or tai' chi).
- Become an author, poet or explore new activities.
- Think more positive.
- Access free medical education.
- Experience a heightened consciousness otherwise healthy people might overlook.
- Become a learned resource for others.

What are my benefits to being sick?

*"Health is a state of complete physical, mental and
social well-being, and not merely the absence
of disease or infirmity."*

~ World Health Organization, 1948

❧ *W*inter ❧
Day Eight

That Takes the Biscuit – The Whole Biscuit

Chronic pain disrupts the harmony of our overall well-being. It is difficult to unlearn certain behaviors. We can if we recognize OUR BODY is injured. When we can see our pain from a different perspective, for instance, as we would a wounded animal, we learn to treat ourselves with the same courtesy.

Equally important is to treat ourselves as a complete being: not half, not one arm or one leg, the whole biscuit, gravy and all. We are each unique in our pain experience, but this we share in common. Striving for balance, treating ourselves with the same respect we would like from others, or give to others, is what helps us preserve as much function as possible and ensures well-rounded emotional, mindful, and spiritual soundness.

Am I looking at myself as the whole biscuit?

19

Mapping my way through life is a road trip
rooted in the lens of my camera.

~ Celeste

❧ *Winter* ❧
Day Nine

Therapy in the Company of Pain
Acupuncture

The ancient Chinese therapeutic approach, acupuncture, is practiced by strategically inserting needles in specific meridians (maps) to unblock the path and stimulate the flow of qi. Doing this balances the disharmony in the body.

The predetermined meridians circulate energy and the acupuncture points are believed to stimulate release of chemicals into the muscles, spinal cord, and brain. These chemicals either change the perception of pain or release other chemicals and hormones that influence the body's ability to create a check and balance system.

Many people testify to the benefits of acupuncture in treating their painful conditions. Success depends on the skills of the practitioner, so we suggest you find a practitioner who has been recommended by several successfully treated patients with conditions similar to your own.

Thanks to continued research on this ancient Chinese therapeutic approach to treating pain and disease, acupuncture is making its way into mainstream healthcare.

Is acupuncture something I might consider to help my pain?

Notes

ॐ

*"He has achieved success who has worked well,
laughed often, and loved much."*

~ Elbert Hubbard, American writer,
publisher, artist, and philosopher, 1856 – 1915.

❧ *Winter* ❧
Day Ten

Word Energy
Recognizing the Power of Words

Changing how we think and how we respond to others can have a powerful impact on our internal search engine. Our descriptive words and reactions for life's ups and downs can influence the contrast between daylight and dark.

Here's an exercise for expanding your search engine.

What do you experience when you:

- Think of the word peace?
- Think of the word pain?

- Think of the word silence?
- Think of the word commotion?

- Think of the word comfort?
- Think of the word conflict?

How did these opposing words affect me differently?
What can I do to change my word energy?

25

*"There is vitality, a life force, an energy, a quickening
that is translated through you into action, and because
there is only one of you in all of time, this expression is
unique. And if you block it, it will never exist through
any other medium and it will be lost."*

~ Martha Grahm, 1894 – 1991,
pioneer of modern dance.

❧ *W*inter ❧
Day Eleven

Words in the Company of Pain
Are Thoughts and Behaviors Making You an Ineffective
Defender?

Unhelpful mechanisms we develop for defense:

- Accusing or blaming.
- Aggressiveness.
- Arguing or tantrums.
- Avoidance or passiveness.
- Compensation – making up for a weakness by excelling in another area.
- Compromise.
- Complaining.
- Confusion.
- Denial.
- Isolation.
- Projection – attributing one's thoughts or impulses to another person.
- Rationalization of the illogical.
- Regression.
- Suppression, intentional denial of thoughts.

Defense mechanisms I identify are...

*"Your pain is the breaking of the shell that
encloses your understanding."*

~ Khalil Gibran, 1883 – 1931, author of
The Prophet, Jesus, The Son of Man, and more...

❧ *W*inter ❧
Day Twelve

Mind Reading

Chronic pain can blur rational thought. At these times, do you rely on others? I do.

Most people are afraid of analyzing others, especially those close to them and especially if that critique suggests our partner is not "up to snuff." The rule of thumb to consider is, if our roles were reversed, would I be grateful for the intercession?

There's a story of a general introducing his new military seaplane to the press. After takeoff, he assumes control and prepares to land at the local airport. The pilot panics but skillfully asks, "General, as this is a seaplane it might be more impressive to land on water and taxi to the dock (full of reporters & photographers)." The general agrees and lands smoothly. At the dock he turns to the pilot and says, "Thank you for correcting my blunder so tactfully, I could have killed us both," and steps out of the plane into the water.

I will be grateful for constructive critiques and make every effort not to see them as criticism.

29

"What we see depends mainly on what we look for."

~ John Lubbock, author of
The Pleasures of Life, The Use of Life*, and more…*

❧ *Winter* ❧
Day Thirteen

Pictures Say a Thousand Words

Pain has a way of narrowing our world. Chronic disease and limitations may leave us with little appreciation of life, beauty, history, and memory. The same experiences of happiness and the possibilities we yearn for in our dreams are available in our compromised conscious life through our deliberate efforts.

Our photos and mementos are just as important in our troubled state of being as they ever were, maybe more. Everyone who has framed or displayed a photo is traveling in time and appreciates the effect. Wisdom tells us that grasping the past is like holding water in our hands.

Appreciate your life; be grateful for your history. Life is a diminishing thing for everyone. Success is recognizing our gratitude and building on it daily.

Are my favorites smothering in an old shoebox? I will dig them out, and enjoy a walk down memory lane.

How does freeing memories make me feel?

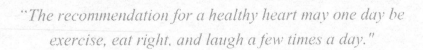

*"The recommendation for a healthy heart may one day be
exercise, eat right, and laugh a few times a day."*

~ Michael Miller, MD,
University of Maryland Medical Center

❧ *W*inter ❧
Day Fourteen

Therapy in the Company of Pain
The Art of Moving

Exercise maintains and improves joint mobility and muscle strength. It also improves the body's endurance and relieves tension. This may be difficult for some of us for various medical reasons, but movement of any kind is something we can do even from a chair if necessary.

Types of exercise:

isometric = sustained contraction with equal opposing force, such as putting your palms together and pushing to create contraction of the pectoral (chest) muscles. It can be done sitting.

weight bearing = exercise with weights to cause contraction of specific muscles. You can also use your own body; an example would be a push up.

aerobic = sustained activity that increases oxygen demand and heart rate. This one requires movement. Start low and go slow.

bouncing = bouncing has been found to not only be an effective form of movement, but can also help with balance and is easy on joints.

rocking chair = rocking can be an important part of health because it improves circulation, increasing blood flow to nerves and other organs of the body. It also helps move lymph fluid, which carries cellular trash out of the body.

What kind of movement can I incorporate into my day?

Notes

ॐ

"No pain, no palm; no thorns, no throne; no gall, no glory; no cross, no crown."

~ William Penn, 1644 – 1718

❧ *Winter* ❧
Day Fifteen

Role Modeling for Universal Love

"A friend is a person with whom I may be sincere. Before him, I may think aloud. I am arrived at last in the presence of a man so real and equal, that I may drop even those undermost garments of dissimulation, courtesy, and second thought, which men never put off, and may deal with him with the simplicity and wholeness with which one chemical atom meets another."

~ Ralph Waldo Emerson

When Emerson's friend Henry David Thoreau was jailed for not paying taxes (as a conscientious objector to the unjust Mexican War), he was looking out of his jail cell on Concord's main street. Emerson saw him in passing and exclaimed, "David, what are you doing in THERE?" Thoreau responded, "Ralph, what are you doing out THERE?" The honesty and focus of their shared love of nature, literature, liberty, and spiritual growth cultivated some of the most influential thinking in our recent history. The courage it takes to be a true friend cannot be over emphasized.

"*People may doubt what you say,*
but they always believe what you do."

~ Anonymous

❧ *Winter* ❧
Day Sixteen

Advocating for Pain
Algology, What?

Algology = *the science and study of pain.*

International Association for the Study of Pain (IASP) = the world's largest multidisciplinary society established to focus specifically on pain research and treatment.

PAIN® is the official publication of the International Association for the Study of Pain.

American Academy of Pain Medicine = the medical specialty society to ensure the comprehensive evaluation and treatment of the pain patient.

The Pain Action Alliance to Implement a National Strategy, PAINS, is an initiative of the Center for Practical Bioethics. Participants of this effort collaborate to implement the Institute of Medicine Report, "*Relieving Pain in America: A Blueprint for Transforming Prevention, Care, Education, and Research.*"

http://PAINSproject.org

What organizations or advocates could I add to this list?

*"Creativity is not bound by the constraints of rationality.
It breaks free through dreams, desire, and imagination."*

~ Deepak Chopra, MD, author of
***The Seven Spiritual Laws of Success,
Reinventing the Body, Resurrecting the Soul***, and more...

❧ *Winter* ❧
Day Seventeen

Finger Painting Is Not For the Faint of Heart

Do you remember what it felt like to put your fingers in paint and freely make drawings without regard to rules or regulations? You can experience it again and the freedom to touch your creative side, discover tactile pleasures, and experience feelings associated with creativity that mean something to you personally.

Discover what makes your creativity tic. Could it be that you enjoy building sand castles, writing in the dirt, or making a scrapbook? Is it building a snowman, or do you find yourself drawing doodle art? Break free of preconceived notions of what creativity is for you. When you do this, you find that special and spiritual pleasure.

What can I do to color up my world today?

"What good is the warmth of summer, without the cold of winter to give it sweetness."

– John Steinbeck, author of **Travels with Charley: In Search of America**, and more...

❧ *Winter* ❧
Day Eighteen

Terms in the Company of Pain
Comfort Foods and the Glycemic Index

Winter is a natural time for energy conservation. The desire for comfort food is instinctive, but seldom a good choice. This season is filled with holidays celebrated around food. Many of the dishes of the festivities aren't always healthy. This is why we should raise our awareness regarding certain foods and the affect they have on our body function.

> High glycemic diets are high in sugar (glucose).

The glycemic index measures how fast a food raises the sugar content in our blood and how quickly our body responds. A high glycemic index diet raises the amount of sugar circulating in our blood, called blood sugar. This creates undue stress on the body, particularly when there is no nutritional value. When we eat foods high in sugar content or foods that quickly convert to sugar (such as complex, high-density carbohydrates), insulin production increases and promotes storage of fat.

Low-density carbohydrates, such as most fruits and vegetables are nutritionally sound and provide vitamins,

43

fiber, and the energy our cells and brain need to be healthy
The higher density, complex carbohydrates mentioned above include foods such as pasta, bread, bagels, desserts, and cereal. Like sugar, they raise blood sugar quickly resulting in surges of insulin release followed by a crash in energy, something already in short supply.

Proteins take longer to utilize and decrease surges in blood sugar and insulin production. Therefore, it lowers our glycemic index, which helps our body stay on an even keel.

Another consideration and a topic of debate is gluten in your diet. Some people tolerate it well and some have Celiac disease or intolerance to gluten. You can read more about Gluten in the *Spring Devotions*.

Eating a balanced meal is important. If you do splurge, try to keep it to a minimum and really enjoy every morsel.

How can I make healthy substitutions this winter?

Notes

ॐ ॐ ॐ

We become who we think we should be.

~ Celeste

❧ Winter ❧
Day Nineteen

How Do I Manage Chronic Pain on a Daily Basis?
The Fifth Vital Sign

Managing pain is not simply treating pain, because when it becomes chronic, pain loses its job as an alarm.

Knowing the root cause (injury, surgery, deformity, or a disease process) doesn't always result in resolution of the fifth vital sign "pain." Messages are interpreted differently by the brain that becomes hyper-vigilant, like a guard waiting for an invasion. It doesn't get a break, goes without sleep, and doesn't experience a period of rejuvenation. The guard can only defend for so long before other factors are immersed in the pain experience. So how can we help?

- Keep a log such as the chart on *Day Thirty*.
- Identify tools you have found helpful.
- Describe pain by painting a picture with a self-drawing (See Day Thirty-seven) or with words.
- Identify behaviors that make pain worse, including social engagements, boredom, or ineffective coping skills such as those found on *Day Eleven*.

What tools could I find helpful to ease the burden on my brain?

47

"Obstacles are those frightful things you see when you take your eyes off the goal."

~ Hannah Moore, 1745 – 1833, poet and author of
Religion of the Heart, 'Tis all for the Best, and more...

❧ *W*inter ❧
Day Twenty

Nice to Meet You, How Do I Do?

Brainfog can be a side effect of chronic pain when pain interferes with sleep. And lack of sleep can aggravate pain.

A good tool for keeping us focused and helping us prioritize is the "To Do" list. We may find what we thought was important either resolves on its own or becomes less of a priority than we originally thought it would be. By having a list, we can write things down and lay it aside at night rather than playing it over and over in our head like a broken record. After all is said and done, nothing can be accomplished unless we get some rest.

My "To Do List"

....

....

....

....

How DO I do?

I could incorporate a "To Do List" section in my journal.

Love is infinite; I will bestow it and accept it.

~ Celeste

❧ Winter ❧
Day Twenty-one

Life Can Be a Daring Adventure

Have you ever heard that old saying, "actions speak louder than words?" They do. Try adding positive verbs to your vocabulary. Action phrases might include:

- Accentuate positives.
- Participate in self–help therapies.
- Join a support network.
- Celebrate accomplishments.
- Support a friend.
- Accomplish my goals.
- Read a self–help book.
- Forgive someone.
- Strive for balance and self–awareness.
- Admire a positive role model.
- Write and read affirmations regularly.
- Activate good nutritional habits.
- Walk.
- Love.

I will drag out a dictionary and learn new verbs to add to my phrases.

"Sometimes I sits and thinks, and sometimes I just sits."

— R. Crumb, American cartoonist

❧ *W*inter ❧
Day Twenty-two

Therapies in the Company of Pain
Types of Movement

range of motion (ROM) = ROM exercises are ones that move each joint through its full normal range of movement. As an example, the knee is a hinge type joint, so normal range of motion would include being able to hold your ankle in your hand and bringing your heel to your buttock, then being able to straighten your leg so that your foreleg is in the same plane as your upper leg. Knee surgery, for instance, causes restrictions and the goal of physical therapy is to restore normal ROM.

active exercise = motion imparted to a body part by willful voluntary contraction and relaxation of its controlling muscles. It is exercise like lifting weights, yoga, walking, and swimming, bouncing, rocking in a chair, or doing jumping jacks.

passive exercise = motion imparted to a segment of the body by another person, machine, or other outside force. Passive motion may also be achieved by voluntary effort of another segment of your own body. An example is raising your left arm with your right arm without any assistance of the left arm muscles. Your left arm experiences passive exercise.

"Remember, no one can make you feel inferior
without your consent."

~ Eleanor Roosevelt

❧ *W*inter ❧
Day Twenty-three

Whole Heartedness

Whatever you do today, do it with your whole heart. Find your strength in giving without reservation. Hold nothing back. Keep your eyes and ears alert to a sad voice or physical expression. Unconditionally offer up your best face in return, whether you feel like it or not. You have the power to make a difference in the life of someone you touch today and that is a gift of selflessness.

I will give the gift of selflessness and in return, I will award myself with a "thumbs up" at the end of the day.

*"Too many people miss the silver lining
because they're expecting gold."*

~ Maurice Setter, Football player and couch

❧ *Winter* ❧
Day Twenty-four

The Ultimate Place

Today describe your ideal place to live. Make it a place that is absent of chaos or woes.

Ask questions of yourself like:

- Would this place keep me warm?
- Would this place give me a sense of awe?
- Would this place make me feel serene?
- Would this place have a cozy fire or a warm bright sky?
- Would this place be decorated with my favorite things?
- Would this place include family, friends, or pets?
- Would this place have a rippling stream or a field of my favorite flowers?

Feel the ambiance, smell the scents, and feel the textures. Describe the surroundings. Steal this moment in time.

I will meditate about my ideal place right now. Close my eyes and breathe in, envision my place, feel my respirations and heart rate decrease as I relax into my place and discover all it has to offer.

Now I will write about my experience or record it so I can play it back in the future.

National Procrastination Day *has been postponed*
due to unforeseen difficulties.

~ Jeff

❧ *Winter* ❧
Day Twenty-five

Procrastinate, Dear Me

Procrastination is something we do when we want to put something off. We postpone action, sometimes until an important opportunity is lost.

In psychology, procrastination refers to the act of replacing high-priority actions with tasks of lower priority, or doing something from which one derives pleasure.

We all know the temptation to do nothing, and we know the temptation to do something more appealing and unnecessary instead of fulfilling an obligation to others or ourselves. It's when we procrastinate or never acknowledge priorities that it becomes a real problem.

You can read more on procrastination in the *Summer Devotions* of this series.

Today I will not procrastinate.

"To insure good health: Eat lightly, breathe deeply,
live moderately, cultivate cheerfulness,
and maintain an interest in life."

~ William Londen, French nature lover

❧ Winter ❧
Day Twenty-six

Treatment in the Company of Pain
Coenzyme Q10

Coenzyme Q10 is a natural compound produced by the body. On a basic cellular level, this antioxidant helps convert food into energy, something those of us with chronic pain wish worked better. Research tells us that pain not only affects us physically and emotionally, but it also has an impact on the way our brain deciphers information and the way our brain assists our body in achieving and maintaining balance. Some think Co-Q 10 helps with brainfog.

Some also believe Co-Q 10 may play a role in keeping cholesterol-lowering statin drugs from depleting our body's natural coenzyme Q10. Studies are underway regarding the effects of Co-Q 10 as a supplement and its usefulness when co-administered with cholesterol lowering drugs.

Beneficial effects, prolonged use, and appropriate dosing are questions that still need to be answered.

"Music in the soul can be heard by the universe."

~ Lao Tzu, Father of Taoism

❧ *Winter* ❧
Day Twenty-seven

You are FULL OF IT!

Thoughtfulness comes in many sizes, shapes, and colors. It becomes tangible when we describe it with metaphors. You can experience it any time day or night. Human goodness, when expressed in thoughtful exchange, has the ability to create a ripple effect.

> *"Do not wait for leaders; do it alone, person to person."*
> ~Mother Teresa

Expressing gratitude is universal. Examples:

- Your thoughtfulness has guided my day and touched my heart.
- Without your caring words and encouragement, I would have had a meltdown.
- Your thoughtfulness touched my soul and renewed my faith.
- Your thoughtfulness was an unselfish act that I shall cherish forever.
- Your caring has changed my life, and I hope it has changed yours too.

My thoughtfulness affirmation for today is…

"There are thoughts which are prayers.
There are moments when, whatever the posture
of the body, the soul is on its knees."

--Victor Hugo, 1802 – 1885,
Literary and political personality of his time,
author of **Les Misérables,** and more...

❧ *W*inter ❧
Day Twenty-eight

Prayer: A Form of Meditation

Prayers are a form of meditation and can provide the same benefits.

Writing our own personal prayer, like writing poetry, raises our awareness of others and ourselves. This form of expression enhances our spiritual awareness.

Prayers often include:

- Thanks/Gratitude
- Repentances/Declarations
- Victory/Triumph
- Requests/Desires
- Comfort/Help
- Forgiveness/Pardon
- Contemplations/Reflections
- Purpose/Reason
- Reinforcement/Support
- Lessons/Teachings
- Praise/Honor
- Testimony/witness

Today I will write a prayer to call my own.

"Pay attention to your body. The point is everybody is different. You have to figure out what works for you."

~ Andrew Weil, MD.
author and Health and Wellness Expert

⤳ *W*inter ⤳
Day Twenty-nine

Nutrition in the Company of Pain
Balancing Your pH

Having an over acidic biological state can create a host of problems. It interferes with the body's ability to absorb important nutrients and minerals. It can aggravate conditions such as gastric reflux, immune deficiency, leaky gut syndrome, and even chronic pain.

Acid = a pH below 7.0

Alkaline (base) = a pH above 7.0

Ideal blood pH in the human body = 7.35 – 7.45

One way of obtaining a proper acid/base balance is through diet. In general, meats, poultry, legumes, eggs, processed and fermented foods, sugar, and fish are considered acid forming foods, while most green vegetables and fruits, tomatoes, avocados, bell peppers, and some seeds and nuts are considered alkaline forming foods. Raw foods are in general more alkalizing, while cooked foods are more acidifying.

We need both acidifying and alkalizing foods to bring balance to the body. The particular balance for you depends upon whether you are maintaining balance or restoring balance. If you are having difficulties with your symptoms, you should consider a consultation with a nutritionist, a physician that specializes in naturopathic medicine, or someone recommended by your personal physician.

There are some good books written on this topic. Check your local library or favorite book resource for more information. Reading the reviews is always helpful.

A healthy pH helps your body operate at an optimal state. Find more information on nutrition on *Day Sixty-nine* and information on how to keep a food calendar in *Spring Devotions.*

I would like to consider how foods might affect my body's balance by:

Notes

ॐ

_____

_____

_____

_____

_____

_____

_____

_____

_____

_____

_____

_____

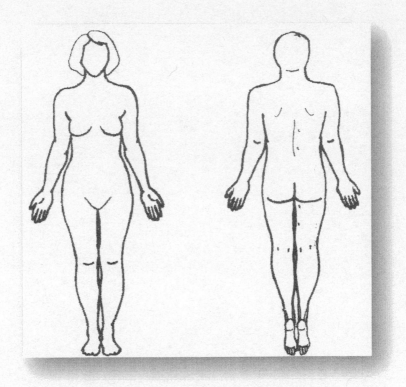

"As a registered nurse and consumer health advocate, I emphatically say that patients are the most important part of the medical team."

~ Barbara Ficarra, RN, BSN, MPA.
Founder Healthin30.com, Award-Winning Broadcast Journalist,
Featured Writer for **The Huffington Post**,
Sharecare Editorial Advisory Board

❧ *Winter* ❧
Day Thirty

You are the Pianist in Your Heath Care
Is Your Piano in Tune?

Name   Date

Treatments have provided:

No relief   Complete Relief

0%   20%   40%   60%   80%   100%

Medications have provided:

No relief   Complete Relief

0%   20%   40%   60%   80%   100%

New coping strategies have provided:

No relief   Complete Relief

0%   20%   40%   60%   80%   100%

(Use this tool periodically for comparison.)

What cords do I need to tune up?

How would I rate my pain in general over the last week?

"Life isn't about finding yourself.
Life is about creating yourself."

~ George Bernard Shaw, 1856 – 1950,
Pygmalion, Fabian, and more…

❧ Winter ❧
Day Thirty-one

POETRY Warms the Heart and Serves the Soul

Ten reasons to write a poem:

1. To express our inner feelings.
2. To honor someone.
3. To celebrate.
4. To work through grief.
5. To observe the world.
6. To open our heart.
7. To express love.
8. To tell a story.
9. To unleash our gratitude.
10. To give as a gift.

Tips: (other tips can be found at www.TheseThree.com)

See the poem on *Day Thirty-eight*. It was inspired by a road trip filled with history near Colorado's Taylor Reservoir. Note the adjectives, nouns, adverbs, and verbs. At times, I use random words from a novel, a book on birds or flowers, or a local paper. Inspiration can come from many sources.

Is there something here I would like to explore?

"You must take personal responsibility. You cannot change the circumstances, the seasons, or the wind, but you can change yourself."

~ Jim Rohn, motivational speaker and author
of ***My Philosophy for Successful Living,***
The Art of Exceptional Living, and more...

❧ *Winter* ❧
Day Thirty-two

Life 101: The Syllabus

Chronic pain and illness can deconstruct relationships with others and with self, so we must do things to affect a positive change in our lives, to learn to love again, and to put these side effects of chronic illness in the past where they belong.

Ten rules for an inspirational life:

1. Stop negative self-talk.
2. Smile at someone and yourself every day.
3. Tell somebody, even a pet, you love him or her.
4. Get control of your short fuse.
5. Identify and focus on strengths.
6. Own your mistakes don't let them own you.
7. Don't pretend to read someone else's mind.
8. Your partner needs support too.
9. Embrace your differences.

Rule #10 – LOVE YOU

Today I will commit to at least one rule.

*"In the midst of winter, I finally learned that there was
in me an invincible summer."*

~ Albert Camus, Nobel Prize winning author
of **The Stranger, The Plague, Notebooks**, and more…

❧ *Winter* ❧
Day Thirty-three

Memories

Our brain has the impressive ability to store and catalogue information from our past. Even more amazing is that we can associate feelings surrounding our memories and resurrect our senses.

Remembering:

- The music of a falling star.
- The earth echoing its presence in the universe.
- A grin on a grandfather's face.
- A baby's first coo.
- The rushing wind howling with a coyote.
- A stranger that touches a soul.
- Gatherings in song.
- The book written for many that spoke only to you.
- Where you played as a child.
- A first friend.
- A first love.
- The sun as it rises over the sea.
- A favorite sunset.
- The indwelling power that comes with an impending storm.
- Stolen moments spent in inspiring thoughts.

Today I will remember three powerful influences in my life.

To fear pain is to deny life because without pain,
one can't recognize pleasure.

~ Celeste

❧ *W*inter ❧
Day Thirty-four

Terms in the Company of Pain
Somatic

The somatic nervous system (SNS), also known as the voluntary nervous system, is part of the peripheral nervous system (PNS). It is responsible for relating motor and sensory information between the brain and spinal cord, the central nervous system, and parts of the body.

> Other effects of the central nervous system are discussed in the *Fall Devotions*. (See about the books in the final pages.)

The nerves of the somatic nervous system join to the skin, sensory organs and all skeletal muscles to create a messaging network that affects almost all voluntary, non–reflex muscle movement. When we choose to move, reach for something on a shelf, our somatic nervous system is responsible. It gives us the ability to contract and relax skeletal muscles for walking, smiling, kicking, swallowing, etc.

The somatic nervous system is also a messaging system for our senses, hearing, sight, taste, touch, and smell. For instance, we know the difference between a light feather touch and the prick of a needle. Damage to nerves in the somatic nervous system, say from nerve impingement in the spine, can interrupt normal sensation and cause numbness.

The somatic nervous system consists of two special types of neurons (nerves cells). One is the sensory (afferent) nerve cell responsible for carrying messages to the brain and spinal cord from muscles and sensory organs. The second is the efferent nerve cell, which carry messages from the brain to muscles. It is a two-way communication interstate.

Why is this important for someone with chronic pain to know?

The somatic nervous system plays a big role in pain. There are two points of importance. First, voluntary movement creates the release of natural painkillers called endorphins (discussed in *Summer Devotions.*)

> **soma** = Greek word for body.
>
> **somatic** = pertaining to a characteristic of the body.

Second, the term "somatic" can be confusing because it translates as body. This term is also used to diagnose mental health disorders such as, earlier "Somatoform Disorders," present "Somatic Symptoms Disorder (SSD)."

Previously, these *somatic symptoms* (complaints about the body) could only be related to mental illness after a physical problem, disease, illness, or injury was considered. That is no longer the case, and this change has many healthcare providers concerned, especially those who treat chronic pain. These healthcare providers fear their patients will be incorrectly diagnosed with *Somatic Symptoms Disorder*, delaying appropriate treatments. The sooner a physical cause of chronic pain can be identified, the more likely the patient will experience a better outcome.

The Diagnostic and Statistical Manual of Mental Disorders is published by the American Psychiatric Association in an effort to classify, diagnose, and gather data on mental illness. The fifth edition (DSM-5), published in 2013, no longer requires that a physical problem be ruled out before diagnosing the patient with *"Somatic Symptom Disorder."*

"While addressing mental health is just as important as diagnosing physical illness, inaccurately diagnosing someone with SSD can cause problems with obtaining insurance, being placed on medications that could create harmful drug interactions, and delaying treatment of physical symptoms. Maintaining mental health is an imperative goal for coping effectively with chronic pain, but in most cases this can be addressed by talk therapy and does not automatically give reason to diagnose a severe mental illness like somatic symptom disorder."

(Excerpt, *Integrative Therapies for Fibromyalgia, Chronic Fatigue Syndrome, and Myofascial Pain: the Mind-Body Connection* covers mental health, depression with chronic pain and the differences between situational and major depression. You can learn more "about the books" at http://www.TheseThree.com)

"Age wrinkles the body. Quitting wrinkles the soul."

~ Douglas MacArthur, 1880 – 1964

❧ *W*inter ❧
Day Thirty-five

Relating Symptoms

Our symptoms indicate a problem somewhere. How we report them to our healthcare professional will improve development of appropriate treatments for us. Follow these tips for relating your symptoms:

onset = When did each symptom or problem begin? Does it happen at a certain time of the day, and what was going on when the symptom/s began?

duration = How long does the symptom last? Is it constant or does it come and go?

severity = How intense is the pain? Are you able to function? Are you able to get to the doctor, or is the pain too severe? Does the pain or other symptoms come in waves of severity? Are you able to complete normal activities of daily living?

character = What does the pain feel like? Is it sharp or dull? Does it stay in the same place, or radiate? Does it feel like needles and pins, or is it completely numb? Is it hot or cold? Describe it. There are *"Terms to Describe Your Symptoms"* on *Day Eighty-four*.

location = What part/s of your body is affected by the symptom or symptoms?

other = How do your symptoms affect your ability to function regarding other aspects of your life, such as your relationships, your emotional state, or your work?

How can I improve the way I relate information to my healthcare providers?

....

....

....

....

....

....

....

Notes

ॐ

"He moved like a dancer, which is not surprising;
a horse is a beautiful animal, but it is perhaps
most remarkable because it moves as
if it always hears music."

~ Mark Helprin, author of **Winter's Tale,**
In Sunlight and in Shadow, and more...

❧ Winter ❧
Day Thirty-six

Terms in the Company of Pain
Pain Threshold

A pain threshold is that level which must be reached for the stimulus to be recognized as painful. This differs for different people. Our personal calibration of one to ten is the point. For example, a one may be a paper cut, or stubbing our toe, and a ten may be a migraine, childbirth, or significant surgical procedure.

Even though I am not a big fan of the 1–10 scale for rating chronic pain, for now, we must learn to live with it.

Determining our own scale related to how chronic pain affects our ability to function will help us and our healthcare providers assess how therapies are working. When we define and share these 'benchmarks," it provides personal, tangible evidence for everyone.

On the 1–10 scale:

What is my one?

What is my ten?

Pain Drawing "Pain'ing"
by Jen Jasper

❧ *Winter* ❧
Day Thirty-seven

You Don't Have to Be A Picasso
Pain'ing and You

A visual aid is a helpful tool for communicating what is not visible to the eye, and drawing about our pain (pain'ing) can be a great self-exploration tool. It can provide deep personal insight. Pain'ing can also help others see what pain means to us while giving us the opportunity to place it outside our body. To share it or not is totally up to you. Keep it in your journal, I have.

The value in placing the awareness outside of our body cannot be overstated. We are simultaneously validating our pain and creating distance so we can be present, but not be enveloped or overwhelmed by pain. This "objectify and observe" approach grants us the tools of external reference and the ability to appreciate incremental improvement.

Our self-drawings, pain'ings, serve as bookmarks in our progress, a visual journal of abiding, adapting, and alleviating.

I will draw a self-caricature of how I feel today.

I started writing to help others,
but what I learn is that I help myself.

~ Celeste

❧ *Winter* ❧
Day Thirty-eight

Ghosts at Taylor Reservoir by Celeste Cooper

Driving the Winding Taylor Canyon Road,
Late August teases of tales to be told.

Giant pines grace roads through this land.
Forest shadows retreat, a reservoir at hand.

Man made, Taylor reservoir feeds the crops,
But once, so much more on this mountain top.

Peering voyeurs of past remnants and such,
This land, bare bones, a boom that went bust.

Tailings at Tin Cup scream loud with their voice.
Tarry you will, but this land was our choice.

Ancient gravesites, ghost tales of lore,
Make great stories when done with the chores.

Sheer splendor tugs at my heartstring,
Cottonwood Pass, the tales you bring.

Time walks on these forest floors,
Taylor River, canoes, Ute Indians explored.

Ancestors relished this county as host,
To share pieces of forest, relics, and ghosts.

Notes for Self-Drawing – Pain'ing

ॐ ॐ ॐ

Stick figures work or cut out features from a magazine that expresses your pain. Convey your "Pain'ing" freely.

Notes for A Poem or Self Reflection

ॐ

Write a poem. Poetry does not have to rhyme, in free style poetry nothing does. (See *Day Eighty-eight*). Just jot down some thoughts and random favorite words. Most of those who write poetry will tell you—the freedom is what gives us a sense of we are. Get started!

*Regret for the things I did not do could someday leave
me broken hearted, for this reason, I try.*

~ Celeste

❧ *W*inter ❧
Day Thirty-nine

"Wait" Control

Many people find short intervals of waiting to be taxing. The issues we have with time centers on our insistence of having "enough" time to complete a job or project. Instead, we have these little gifts of minutes that can be as useful as collecting change in a jar. In themselves, they may seem insignificant, but overall they create a large opportunity made from small components. This is where I give my impatient friends a magazine (*Prevention, Reader's Digest, The Sun, Tricycle, The Week*, for example) and demonstrate how five minutes can be profitably invested. Clear your "To Do" list or learn something new.

Don't miss the opportunity to divert your attention from pain and/or fatigue. Time spent waiting is precious— time we might otherwise miss. When we view waiting time as an opportunity to clean up unpleasant thoughts from our cerebral real estate, we can look forward to these little gifts of time.

Next time I am pushed into wait mode, I will see it as an opportunity, a gift of time.

"There are no failures—only learners."

~ Buckminster Fuller, 1895 - 1983.
Presidential Medal of Freedom and author of
Critical Path, A Fuller Explanation: The Synergetic Geometry,
and many more...

❧ *Winter* ❧
Day Forty

Writing Your Own Hobby Resume

Hobbies can be a great diversion. They can motivate us and create feelings of joy and accomplishment. We may have to suffer the learning curve, but that only intensifies the reward.

Questions for writing a hobby resume:

- What are your work experiences?
- Is there a particular skill you can apply to a hobby?
- What's something you always wanted to do, but didn't?
- How might you expand or reinvent a hobby you love by changing the elements to meet your present limitations?
- Have you mentored others on your hobby?
- What is your hobby network?
- Do you subscribe to magazines regarding your hobby?
- What are your plans for expanding or reinventing your hobby?
- Where might you look for a new hobby?

How can I use my hobby resume to expand my thoughts, explore new desires, or resurrect old ones?

"A ship in the harbor is safe.
But that's not what ships are built for."

~ John A. Shedd,
author of **Salt from My Attic**

❧ *W*inter ❧
Day Forty-one

Advocacy: Promoting Purpose

The building blocks of advocacy are raising public awareness, promoting research funding, obtaining proper treatment, and asking for adequate support from family and friends.

You might accomplish this by:

- Joining an organization that is passion specific.
- Networking with others who have similar interests.
- Sharing information with those who want to help you.
- Writing letters to organizations that provide research for chronic pain disorders.
- Becoming politically active.

More information and helpful links available at
http://TheseThree.com

"My old grandmother always used to say,
summer friends will melt away like summer snows,
but winter friends are friends forever."

~ George R.R. Martin, author of
A Feast for Crows, The Hedge Night, and more...

❧ *W*inter ❧
Day Forty-two

Count Your Blessings

"But oh! the blessing it is to have a friend to whom one can speak fearlessly on any subject; with whom one's deepest as well as one's most foolish thoughts come out simply and safely. Oh, the comfort - the inexpressible comfort of feeling safe with a person - having neither to weigh thoughts nor measure words, but pouring them all right out, just as they are, chaff and grain together; certain that a faithful hand will take and sift them, keep what is worth keeping, and then with the breath of kindness blow the rest away."

~ Dinah Craik, A Life for a Life, 1859

Recognizing positive attributes of significant others in our life, such as a soft place to lay our head; share our triumphs and struggles; appreciate a certain look, a wink, or the sweetness of a hug, fuels a friendship that will last a lifetime.

My blessings are:

1) _____

2) _____

3) _____

The power of physical, emotional, mental and
spiritual balance is achieved by being mindful.
Whether in sorrow or joy, in pain or triumph, striving
for this awareness makes the journey a full one.

~ Celeste

❧ *Winter* ❧
Day Forty-three

Express Yourself: What, Where, When, Why

We have talked about what, where, and when related to symptoms. Now it is important to understand the "why." When we are vague, it can be misleading.

Following are examples:

"I feel exhausted." How do you come to this conclusion? Are you unable to get out of bed? Are you unable to complete personal hygiene? Or, are you simply a little off?

"I can't function." Why are you unable to function? Has your pain level increased? Has the location and character of your pain changed, and if so, how? Are you unable to concentrate? Are you unable to complete tasks that are normally easy for you? If so, explain why.

Our healthcare provider should want to know how our pain affects us mentally, emotionally, and spiritually, not just physically. So, next time you make notes for your healthcare provider appointment, keep this in mind. Paint a picture of how you have improved or declined by explaining the "why."

I will keep the "why" in mind when relating my symptoms.

Looking back ten years, knowing how I feel today,
I appreciate the now because in ten years I will look back
and remember these days as the good days.

~ Celeste

❧ *Winter* ❧
Day Forty-four

The Gift of Time

> "For when you are seventy years old and look back at what your life has meant, you will not focus on your solo activities.
>
> What you will remember are the incidents of touching, those times when your life was enriched by a moment of sharing with a friend or loved one.
>
> It is our mutual awareness of this miracle called life that allows us to accept our mortality."

Excerpt from *Cradle* by A.C.Clarke and G.Lee. NY: Warner Books, 1988.

What will I remember?

Today I will give myself time.

Others can count on me, but like all things real,
I accept accommodations may be necessary.

~ Celeste

❧ *Winter* ❧
Day Forty-five

Is Your Slope Slippery?

Periodic assessments are as important as having snow to build a snowman. Over this past week:

Pain has generally interfered with function:
    barely – somewhat – can't function

Pain has affected my ability to go on outings:
    rarely – somewhat – significantly

My sleep quality has been:
    adequate – Impaired – can't function

I was able to sleep:
    7–9 hours 4–6 hours 2–3 hours

My Concentration/memory is:
    good – decreased – greatly impaired

Can I identify anything that aggravated or alleviated these factors?

How does this compare to last week?

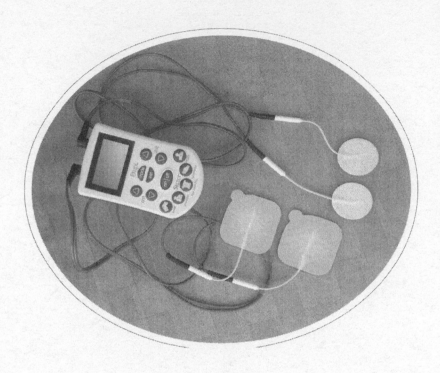

"Man seems to be a rickety poor sort of a thing, any way
you take him; a kind of British Museum of infirmities and
inferiorities. He is always undergoing repairs. A machine
that was as unreliable as he is would have no market."

~ Mark Twain, (Samuel Clemens), 1835 – 1910

❧ *W*inter ❧
Day Forty-six

Only One Nerve Left:
The Use of E-Stim Units for Blocking Pain

E-Stim is short for electrical stimulation. Various types of devices are available for transmitting an electrical pulse via electrodes that attach specialized pads to the skin. Blocking painful impulses, which signal the brain to react, may help divert pain perception.

There are certain health conditions and contraindications for using an electrical stimulation unit so talk with your physician or physical therapist to see if E-Stim might be a viable option for you.

Types of E-Stim units:

- Transcutaneous Electrical Nerve Stimulation (T.E.N.S).
- Micro-current.
- Interferential stimulation units.
- Galvanic stimulation.
- Automated twitch obtaining intramuscular stimulation (ATOIMS).
- Electrical twitch-obtaining intramuscular stimulation (ETOIMS).

*May our spirit fill us with understanding of
victory and defeat, the gift of collaboration,
the wisdom to choose the right path,
and opportunities that inspire hope.*

~ Celeste

❧ *W*inter ❧
Day Forty-seven

Confidence When It Counts

Being able to relate our health needs with confidence is very important and can affect the outcome of what tests might be needed and what treatments might be helpful. Good communication with our doctors is important to ensure a proper diagnosis and receive appropriate referrals to other healthcare team members.

A pain calendar (from a dollar store) can help us keep track of abnormal responses to physical activities, therapies, medication changes, sleep, mental alertness, weather changes, diet changes, or other changes that might affect our symptoms. We can note trends using the tools provided in this book on days, six, thirty, forty-five, and sixty.

We should take our calendar and assessment tools with us to our doctor and healthcare provider visits so they can make adjustments in our treatment when necessary.

There are other helpful tools, such as a medication log, symptoms inventory sheet, anatomical diagram of pain, health history log, diet assessment guide, chronological health record, and more in *Integrative Therapies for*

Fibromyalgia, Chronic Fatigue Syndrome, and Myofascial Pain…

Myofascial pain is a peripheral pain generator in most chronic pain conditions. You can read more about it in the *Spring Devotions.*

Today I will start a pain calendar so I can relate my discomfort to certain factors in my life. Following are some things to remember.

_____

_____

_____

_____

_____

_____

_____

_____

_____

Notes

"Assumptions are the termites of relationships."

~Henry Winkler

❧ *Winter* ❧
Day Forty-eight

Ten Rules for Building Supportive Relationships

Socialization is a basic human need, and healthy relationships are an important part of the socializing process.

Ten tips for building the relationships we all need:

1. Keep information regarding your illness basic.
2. Find ways to avoid isolation.
3. Keep your support structure trustworthy.
4. Maintain a variety of friendships.
5. Construct a strong support system.
6. Don't expect others to read your mind.
7. Ask for patience when you need it.
8. Plan activities or outings.
9. Write a letter of support for someone else. (Share it or save it in your journal.)
10. Don't be a martyr, find your inner hero.

I will find 5 rules to build on and write them on s notes page or in my journal.

"Not everything that is faced can be changed, but nothing can be changed until it is faced."

~James Baldwin, author of
Hero Tales, Another Country, and more...

❧ *Winter* ❧
Day Forty-nine

Counting Your Change

A great little book titled "Who Moved My Cheese" by Spencer Johnson, M.D is about two mice, one who adapts to change, and one who doesn't. The story shows the difference in perception of change and the outcomes as they work through a maze, which is the metaphor for life.

Having a chronic pain condition creates change because pain is more than physical. It's mental, emotional, and spiritual. When we change our perception and behaviors, we can find opportunities that would be lost to us in a pain free life. Every advocate was born from some adversity in either their life or the life of someone dear to them.

Without hardship, there wouldn't be change. When we embrace it, we CAN change, even if our physical situation is static. Seeing change as an opportunity rather than digging in our heels, seeing it as an obstacle to be resisted, teaches us to navigate the maze of chronic pain with mental, emotional, and spiritual success. (See *Spring* and *Summer Devotions* for more information on how to accept change.)

How will I embrace change in my life today and turn it into something I appreciate?

*What I eat affects the way my body functions, it is up to
me to decide how to improve my habits.*

~ Celeste

❧ *W*inter ❧
Day Fifty

Nutrients in the Company of Pain
Probiotics

The bowel is host to many types of bacteria, and sometimes it can be a host to yeast. Various friendly bacteria act as natural killers of potentially harmful bowel organisms.

Keeping the gut healthy is important because that is where nutrients are extracted from what we eat; those nutrients are used for cellular energy and overall health. Digestion rids the body of the metabolic byproduct of food, which is waste. It is suspected that the many preservatives, food colorings, and other chemicals found in and on some foods break down the lining of our intestines, causing holes. The waste extracted from what we eat is toxic and can leak into our bloodstream, wreaking havoc. It affects all our body systems, including those systems that affect our perception of pain. Medications can also interfere with a normal bowel environment, so if you are experiencing symptoms or changes in your bowel function you might want to discuss this with your physician.

The many strains of friendly bacteria, probiotics, have been studied and it appears they are helpful for supporting digestive health.

"The fault of every character comes from not listening."

~David Drake, Vietnam Vet and author of
With the Lightnings, The Road of Danger, and more...

❧ *Winter* ❧
Day Fifty-one

Discovering the Power of Limitations

Complications of pain, isolation, and poor self-esteem suggest we need to approach our blocks to growth with tender loving care and nurture self by making positive change. When we acknowledge these complications, we can begin work on a sound support structure.

Our (allies), our cheerleaders, play an important role in how we respond to the "side effects" of pain. In a healthy relationship, being a cheerleader is mutual. We should expect and accept everyone has limitations. However, knowing when a relationship is constructive or destructive is still important.

Goals for finding power in limitation:

- Strengthen mutually rewarding relationships.
- Identify relationships that require energy.
- Offer support.
- Be prepared to "let go."
- Expect that "cheerleaders" want us to be our best.

What can I do to maintain and build healthy relationships?

*I embrace change because new events help
me savor all the good life has to offer.*

~ Celeste

❧ *Winter* ❧
Day Fifty-two

Are We A Cucumber or A Bag of Chips?

Improper nutrition can be a major perpetuating factor to pain. For instance, a small amount of caffeine is indicated for migraine, and it can help with fatigue. Coffee and green teas contain antioxidants that target free radicals, the culprits that damage cells and interfere with healing. Yet, too much of the many caffeine containing products can cause symptoms such as, gastrointestinal upset, headaches, increased heart rate and blood pressure, and dysfunctional sleep.

A balanced diet is especially important for people in chronic pain. Medications may interfere with nutritional balance, so we must be ever vigilant. Pain also affects our mobility, which can make it difficult to maintain a healthy weight, putting more stress on organs and joints.

There are nutritional guidelines that can minimize the inflammation present in some painful conditions. Pick up a good book or check out the *American Arthritis Foundation*, who offers a great deal of educational material.

I will identify comfort foods, and improve my winter nutritional status.

123

If I plant kindness, I will gather compassion.

~ Celeste

❧ *W*inter ❧
Day Fifty-three

This is YOUR Life: There Are No Reruns

Kindness is the lighthouse that eternally guides our life's journey. There is courage in kindness. The act of devoting self enriches our lives. If we give nothing, we receive nothing. If we receive nothing, we become nothing, and pain will rob us. Life should be more than a waiting period.

Life's kindness:

- Appreciating others' struggles.
- Expressing compassion.
- Offering a hug.
- Appreciating all cultures.
- Being gentle.
- Being thoughtful.
- Considering others feelings.
- Connecting with all humanity.
- Offering goodwill.
- Being supportive, helpful, and friendly.
- Recognizing kindness as a universal language.

Have I thought about my choices?

Where do I envision myself six months from now?

*"You never understand a person until
you consider things from his point of view."*

–Harper Lee, author of
To Kill a Mockingbird

❧ *Winter* ❧
Day Fifty-four

Holding Hands, Touching Hearts

When we reach out to someone or someone reaches out to us, we need to be flexible in what we expect.

It is vital that we nurture relationships that help us explore relationship diversity. When we are able to consider things from another's viewpoint, we learn to appreciate that person's role in our life and benefit from it. We touch hearts when we care enough to listen without preconceived notions or expectations. Variety is the spice in life.

Breaking out of roles of habitual limitations raises our awareness to the assortment of roles others play in our lives and the different roles we play in theirs. How boring would it be if jellybeans were all the same color?

When we connect with a person on this level of acceptance, without judgment, when we reach out, they will take our hand.

Whose heart can I touch today by breaking out of the role of my own limitations?

"To everything there is a season."

~Ecclesiastes 3:1 KJV

❧ *Winter* ❧
Day Fifty-five

Movement Therapy:
Does Your Oil Need to be Changed?

Moving releases natural painkillers from our brain called endorphins. Winter is a time when animals typically slow down, but we cannot afford to do that. We don't have to run a marathon, but we need to move or our muscles will waste, our lymph fluid will become stagnant, and toxins will build up in our body. Now is the time to reeducate our body. Practice provides the repetitive information our brain needs for decreasing pain. We must keep our oil clean.

Gentle movement therapies include:

- Qi gong.
- T'ai Chi.
- Water/aqua therapy.
- Aston patterning.
- Bounce back chair.
- Hatha Yoga and/or Yoga ball.
- Feldenkrais.
- Hellerwork.

- Rocking chair exercise. (See *Spring Devotions.*)
- Stretching.
- Aerobic, passive, and anaerobic exercise.
- Meditative movement.
- The Alexander Technique.
- Somatic movement therapy.
- Rhythmic vibratory movements.

Some of these therapies are discussed in detail in the *Fall, Summer, Winter,* and *Spring Devotions* of the *Broken Body, Wounded Spirit: Balancing the See-Saw of Chronic Pain* series.

How can I change my oil and keep my motor running smoothly?

Notes

ॐ

"Vision without action is a daydream.
Action without vision is a nightmare."

~Japanese Proverb

❧ *Winter* ❧
Day Fifty-six

The Pain Experience: When We Are Trying to Be Still

It's healthy to let our mental faculties have a vacation from daily stressors and productivity. But, what can we do to calm down this process when it wants to take on a mind of its own?

There will be times when pain wants to be boss no matter what we do to ignore it, but there are times when we do have power as negotiator.

Here are some tips:

- It takes practice to be mindful.
- Diversion works so pick up a hobby.
- Guided imagery and meditation are helpful.

You will find that being mindful of your pain, and giving it the tender loving care that it deserves is useful. Negative thoughts regarding pain ramp up parts of our brain that enhance and amplify the pain experience. We will still have these thoughts, but when we learn to acknowledge them without judgment, we omit our negativity.

How can I redirect pain when it gets bossy?

*"When I woke up this morning my girlfriend asked me,
'Did you sleep good?' I said 'No, I made a few mistakes."*

~Steven Wright, comedian

❧ Winter ❧
Day Fifty-seven

Now I Lay Me Down to Sleep
My Personal Testimony

"I am so tired. However, as I resign myself to bed each night I strive to embrace sleep that may or may not come. If I do slumber, I am too often awakened with the feeling that my extremities have been amputated with the ax of a grim reaper. My thrashing about and kicking brings unwelcome remarks from a spouse who swears I am physically abusing him in retaliation for his snoring.

When I get the nerve (literally) to get my feet on the floor, I seldom feel them. When I do, every muscle seems to work against the other, and I pray not to topple until the feeling of the needles in the bottom of my feet passes, pleading that it will pass and the morning hours turn the day into one that is more acceptable. I examine everything I do or do not put into my mouth, from diet to medications, for fear in a few hours my head will feel like I am on a whirlybird, death-drop ride that won't stop. I toil to embrace my body's alarm system. What do I do now...?"

Winter is thought of as a time for hibernation and rest, however for those of us with chronic pain, our body wants to determine otherwise. I now use the useful tips we write about in this book series, and I consult with my doctor for addressing sleep problems.

What can I do to prepare myself before "I lay me down to sleep?"

135

I am more than the sum of my parts,
if I improve on any one thing, I have made
a choice to improve who I am.

~ Celeste

❧ *Winter* ❧
Day Fifty-eight

Supplements in the Company of Pain
Melatonin

Melatonin is a naturally occurring hormone that the body converts into serotonin, and serotonin is a chemical messenger that is thought to be in short supply during chronic pain.

Melatonin is secreted by the pineal gland at the base of the brain, which begins its work in darkness. Levels peak in early morning hours, and start to fall off at sunset, as discussed on *Day Two*.

Questions have been raised regarding supplement safety, potency, purity, and recommended dose. The supplemental use of all hormones should be monitored by your physician. Medication with properties that will encourage the use of our own body's melatonin may prove to be a safer choice.

You can learn more about legitimate safety concerns shared by Dr Mehmet Oz at:
http://www.doctoroz.com/episode/why-melatonin-may-be-dangerous-your-sleep

"Many persons have a wrong idea of what constitutes
true happiness. It is not attained through
self-gratification but through fidelity
to a worthy purpose."

~ Helen Keller

138

❧ *Winter* ❧
Day Fifty-nine

But Travel

by Celeste Cooper

Travel in the darkness
Travel in the sun
Travel in the light of being
But, travel.

What is my worthy purpose?

"Regret for things we did can be tempered by time; it is regret for the things we did not do that is inconsolable."

~Sydney J. Harris, *author of* ***Winners and Losers, Last Things First****, and more...*

❧ *Winter* ❧
Day Sixty

60,000 Mile Warranty

Over the past six months: (circle those that apply)

Pain is:
absent – tolerable – moderate – severe

Activity level is:
good – moderate – poor – very poor

Energy is:
good – moderate – poor – very poor

Sleep quality is:
good – moderate – poor – very poor

Sleep amount is:
2–4 hours   4–6 hours   6–8 hours   9 or more

Feel rested:
always – occasionally – never

Concentration/memory is:
good – moderate – poor – very poor

I will use this tool periodically to evaluate my progress.

"May I be well, happy, and peaceful?"

~Tatianna Pouladian,
Meditation teacher and student

❧ *Winter* ❧

Day Sixty-one

To Dance with Your Inner Being: Waltz or the Twist?

Meditation practice:

- Visualize yourself strolling through the forest.
- Do you see the trees or smell the leaves dusted with snow?
- Can you feel a winter storm approaching?
    o What does the sky look like?
    o What color is it?
    o Is it dotted with clouds?
    o What shape are the clouds?
    o How fast are they moving?
- Are snowflakes licking at your face?
- Is someone walking with you?
- What is beneath your feet?
- What do you see in the distance?
    o Snow capped mountains?
    o A farmhouse?
    o A path that rises to meet the sky?
- Is there a clearing with deer grazing ahead?

I will imagine what I am experiencing with the freedom of mindful creativity.

"Of all the people you will know in a lifetime, you are the only one you will never leave nor lose. To the question of your life, you are the only answer. To the problems in your life, you are the only solution."

~Jo Coudert, author of
Advice From A Failure. GoWell, and more…

❧ *W*inter ❧
Day Sixty-two

Final Analysis, Part I

How ironic it is that when we can count down our final breaths, we have no concern whatsoever for what others think of our person, ideas, and beliefs. Lives once lived secondary to fear of the judgment of others, of fitting in and participating in trends, fashions, and opinions are now freed to experience the folly of their yardsticks.

What is ultimately important is personal integrity. You never leave you. You create and recreate you. You give yourself that final report card and you sign it. Excuses are not pertinent nor are they accepted.

Dignity, integrity, love and commitment are what matter, everything else is confetti swept to the gutters from a parade we can barely remember.

The elements in the "Final Analysis," dignity, integrity, love, and commitment are discussed throughout our books.

In the final analysis, what is my yardstick?

"People come; people go.....life is like that. Accept it.
I am not here to reform the world, but to reform myself.
When I have changed myself, then
I have changed the world."

~ Swami Satchidananda, Yoga Master and author of
To Know Your Self, The Living Gita and more…

❧ *W*inter ❧
Day Sixty-three

When Dealing with a Burned Out Light Bulb,
Change It!

How many psychologists does it take to change a light bulb? Just one, but it takes a long time, costs a lot of money, and the light bulb really has got to want to change.

One of the first questions you should ask your psychologist is what beliefs have been changed in their thinking over the last ten years. Have they changed their own bulbs?

Karma = an Indian religious concept of action or deed, the outcome of our own past and present actions.

Read more in the *Fall Devotions*.

http://www.amazon.com/dp/B009OQJB8I

Dogma = principles set by an authority as undeniably true, the base on which an ideology or belief system is built.

"My karma ran over my dogma"
~Swami Beyondananda

It is fair to expect change for others and myself.

147

As I peel away the crust that encases my pain,
I let go. If even for a moment, my soul is anointed
with a crown of victory, not to be taken lightly,
but held as close as a baby in the womb is.

~ Celeste

✌ *Winter* ✌
Day Sixty-four

Terms in the Company of Pain

allodynia = pain from a stimulus that doesn't usually cause pain.

arthralgia = joint pain; pain where two bones are connected.

causalgia = a constant, usually burning, pain resulting from injury to a peripheral nerve often associated with vasomotor and sweat gland dysfunction. Complex regional pain syndrome is a type of causalgia.

central pain = pain associated with a disruption in the workings of the central nervous system.

dermatome = the segment of skin or subcutaneous tissue supplied with sensory nerve fibers in a particular pattern.

dysesthesia = an unpleasant abnormal sensation.

hyperalgesia = an increased reaction to a stimulus that is normally painful.

hypoalgesia = a decreased reaction to a stimulus that is normally painful.

myalgia = muscle pain.

neuralgia = pain along a nerve track. (Read more in *Fall Devotions*

neuritis = pain from an inflamed nerve.

referred pain = pain in a part of the body different from the point or origin.

sciatica = pain along sciatic nerve track located in the buttocks and the parts of the body it serves.

trigger point = a self-sustaining, irritable area in the muscle that can be felt as a nodule in a taut band. (See *Spring Devotions* in this series for more information.)

Notes

ॐ

"*You are successful the moment you start moving
toward a worthwhile goal.*"

~Charles Carlson, author of
*The Little Book of Big Dividends:
A Safe Formula for Guaranteed Returns
(Little Books. Big Profits)*, and more...

❧ *Winter* ❧
Day Sixty-five

Commit Yourself

Your healthcare team should appreciate the benefits of a patient-proactive-role. Qualify that you want to be a primary member of your healthcare team, and you are willing to accept that responsibility.

Here are some tips for improving communication:

- Find people for your healthcare team that listen.
- Be accountable for your role in your healthcare.
- Be prepared for your appointment.
- Keep a notebook on your health history and medications.
- Evaluate and report to your therapist or physician on the effectiveness of the treatment.
- Discuss how your treatment plan improves or prohibits functioning.
- Expect changes in your treatment plan.
- Develop a rapport with assistive staff members.
- If you feel your healthcare team members are non-communicative, find ones who are.

Find more tips on journaling and affirmations in the other books in this series.

I will take a proactive role in my healthcare.

My life can be described as having peaks and valleys, and ebb and flow. Difficult days can be an abyss or a hurricane, yet other days are a calm eddy. They all prove I share the force of nature.

~ Celeste

❧ *W*inter ❧
Day Sixty-six

The Ebb and Flow of Chronic Pain

Acceptance is the first step to managing chronic pain. It has a profound effect on the way we look at our illnesses. We grieve the person we once were, and so do those around us. When we accept, then we can move on.

Our function has been altered and finding new ways of coping with our losses is important and empowering to us. We should not doubt that we can, instead we should rediscover and redefine who we are. We can do this through journaling, writing affirmations, and focusing on what we can do.

If you are not finding the support you need, see a counselor who is experienced in helping people with chronic pain.

Find tips on journaling and affirmations at:
www.thesethree.com

What steps can I take to embrace the idea that pain is one part of who I am, but it does not define my character?

155

"The currency we have for getting what
we want is the way we think."

–Dr. Wayne Dyer, author of
I AM Wishes Fulfilled Meditation,
Change Your Thoughts, Change Your Life, and more...

❧ *Winter* ❧
Day Sixty-seven

What Is of What Becomes
Success or Failure

Many variables factor into that which is and what it becomes. The most powerful of these is the language of our own thoughts. What we tell ourselves is the single greatest force in our eventual success or failure. Pragmatic, realistic optimism is the best strategy for enjoying life.

Re-evaluating the obvious can be a lifesaver, as in the story about survivors of a plane crash in the wilderness. They had water, shelter, and raw meat. But they only had one match to use to eat or signal for help and no tinder in the damp forest. One survivor fills some time talking about family and brings forth pictures, then realizes that the hundreds of dollars in his billfold is the solution they need.

In this analogy, paper is the fuel to start our fire.
It's about finding the currency to get what we want.

Today I will re-evaluate my currency for success of failure.

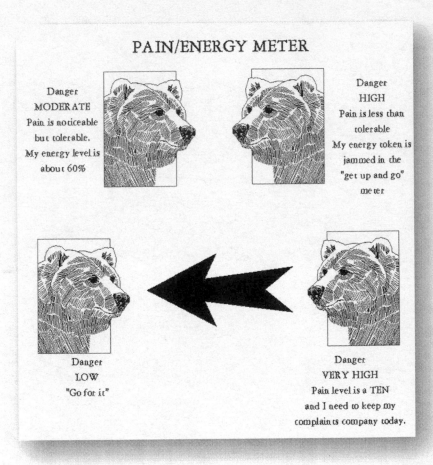

Pain Energy Meter

❧ *Winter* ❧
Day Sixty-eight

Is Your Pain or Energy Meter Running Out of Time?

In nature, winter is a season for saving energy for spring and re-growth. For humans, winter is a time to reflect. The sun's energy is in high demand for those who have seasonal affect disorder. In other words, it is a time when our energy may not be easily supported.

> "There will also be days when your battery is half-drained before your feet hit the floor. Every morning you should check your voltage. If it is low, plan your activity accordingly. Make sure you leave enough 'spark' at the end of the day for overnight reenergizing."

(Excerpt, *Integrative Therapies for Fibromyalgia, Chronic Fatigue Syndrome, and Myofascial Pain* ... Cooper and Miller, Healing Arts Press, 2010. See *about the books* in the final pages.)

Posting our pain and energy meter where our family can access it will let them know if today is a super terrific day, a terrific day, a semi-terrific day, or one where we are just grateful to wake up. They need to know what our energy level is so they can limit requests, and they need to know when we feel like doing things so we can contribute. These things give us value from all perspectives.

I will put a pain energy meter on my refrigerator.

159

"The body is the temple of the soul."

~Dr.Mehmet Oz

❧ *Winter* ❧
Day Sixty-nine

Nutrition in the Company of Pain
The Banana

When dealing with chronic pain issues, it is sometimes difficult to prepare meals. Here is a healthy breakfast or snack solution if you have a blender, or single serving blender device.

Ingredients:

Use fresh and/or frozen fruits and vegetables on hand and add other herbs to your liking. Keep in mind that for some an anti-inflammatory choice is a smart selection, particularly if you are subject to irritable bladder, GERD, immune deficiencies, or leaky gut syndrome.

Did you know that you could freeze a whole banana and use it later? Yes, it is true; you can cut off what you need and easily remove the peeling. Not only do they add flavor, bananas also add fiber, protein, vitamin B6, vitamin C, potassium, manganese, magnesium, folate, riboflavin, niacin, vitamin A, and iron. There is a reason they are considered as a baby's first food.

*If you are sticking to a low acid diet, check books at your local library or resources on the internet to see if other ingredients are "acid forming." They can be acidic, but that does not mean they create an acidic environment in your body. This too requires balance.

THE BANANA IS AN ALKALINE FORMING FRUIT!

What fruits and vegetables would I consider a tasty healthful breakfast or snack?

_____

_____

_____

_____

_____

_____

_____

Notes

ॐ

"Reason is our soul's left hand, Faith her right."

~John Donne, 1572 – 1631, known for his ability to unite,
author of **No Man Is An Island**, founder of the Metaphysical Poets

❧ *W*inter ❧
Day Seventy

Developing the Mind, Soothing the Soul

Developing reason is pretty straightforward. The process consists largely of recognizing our own persistent errors. Nothing is more helpful in this process than a relentless critic is. We should embrace our critic (we all do it) as our fact checker, editor, and purifying flame.

Faith, on the other hand, does not suffer criticism well and the previous helper (critic) now becomes the destroyer. Our ultimate—at this time—belief will lie between two points: thoroughness (rigor) and inflexibility (rigidity). It will agree wholly with neither. Rigor in the inquisitive method is very helpful while rigidity in outcome is not. Every spiritual leader was in his or her day a heretic.

TREAD BRAVELY PILGRAM

I accept that faith is to sooth my soul and sometimes guides me just as well without conscious effort or application.

165

*"Silence is the language God speaks,
and everything else is a bad translation."*

~ Father Thomas Keating,
Popular for centering prayer

166

❧ *W*inter ❧
Day Seventy-one

Terms in the Company of Pain
The suffix of ology

algology = the science and study of pain. (See "Day Sixteen.")

biology = the study of living matter.

etiology = the study of the origin of symptoms

kinesiology = the study of how individual muscle function provides information about a patient's overall health.

neurology = the science and study of the nervous system

pathology = the study of abnormal responses in the body.

pharmacology = the study of medicine to alleviate symptoms and disease.

physiology = the study of how the body works physically.

psychology = the study of behavior.

rheumatology = the study of joints and soft tissue disorders.

"Spiritual realities are the underpinnings, the very template of existence."

~Jean Houston, author of
***The Wizard of Us, The Possible Human,
A Passion for the Possible**,* and more...

❧ *Winter* ❧
Day Seventy-two

Spiritual Realities

Research on faith and healing clearly demonstrates that faith itself and action (e.g. prayer) causes positive change in physical conditions. The type of religious or spiritual practice is not important in obtaining the benefits of emotional acceptance. The balance of spiritual, physical, mental, and emotional existence is what's important.

Dr. Jean Houston is one of the most inspiring, thoughtful and engaging thinkers I have met. She put her PhD in Psychology in her back pocket and got another in Religion before starting a wave in human potential exploration. Jean is a very logical agent for personal transformation along epic and unique lines of thinking. Every life has its' own course and purpose. Failure in her world is failure to dare.

Our spiritual journey offers the beginning of an unfolding map toward our highest potential. No two are alike. . If someone insists his or her path is the only correct one, beware. Buddha said (with his last breath)…

"Be a lamp unto thyself."

"*Mirth is God's medicine. Everybody ought
to bathe in it.*"

~Henry Ward Beecher, author of
***Twelve Causes of Dishonesty and Conflict of Northern
and Southern Theories of Man and Society Great Speech,***
Delivered in New York City

❧ *W*inter ❧
Day Seventy-three

Mirth

Glee – Gaiety – Jollity - Merriment

The Torah states: "*Happy are those who find wisdom.*" Finding a good balance between our physical, mental, emotional, and spiritual nature enlightens us as to who we are as a whole person. When we understand this connection, we develop a profound understanding of mirth.

Is to be wise, to be happy? I think not. I have known many people I consider wise, but I would not say they were gleeful in the traditional sense. So maybe it's more about finding the gaiety in the wisdom, acknowledging that we are meant to grow and learn and to find joyful feelings in that knowledge.

Can we find mirth in our thoughts? The Buddha said, "*We are shaped by our thoughts; we become what we think. When the mind is pure, joy follows like a shadow that never leaves.*" So maybe we should look for purity within ourselves.

In Christianity we are taught, "*The kingdom of heaven is within us.*"

171

Now can you see a trend among the great religions?

Maybe the answer is in finding ways to create our own mirth, to redefine what that is for us individually and find ways to nurture ourselves by acting with glee, gaiety, jollity, and merriment.

How can I find mirth for myself?

_____

_____

_____

_____

_____

_____

_____

_____

_____

_____

Notes

*"Many of life's failures are people who did not realize
how close they were to success when they gave up."*

~ Thomas Edison

❧ *Winter* ❧
Day Seventy-four

At the Root of Anger Are Fears

Gerald Jampolsky, MD makes the case that what is not love IS fear, including anger and judgment, in his excellent short book, Love is Letting Go of Fear. If we see anger for the fear it truly is, then clarity ensues. Fear is harder to endure at first until it is accepted as a phase in a process.

We fear what we don't understand. Acknowledging and accepting fear and educating ourselves on unknowns frees us from the prison of anger.

> *What are my fears?*
>
> *Where does my anger come from?*
>
> *What are my judgments?*

I will use love, acceptance, and understanding to let them go so that I may be free.

175

*"Create your tomorrows with your
thoughts and actions today."*

~Catherine DeVrye, author of
Hope Happens Words of Encouragement for Times of Change,
Hot Lemon and Honey, and more...

❧ *Winter* ❧
Day Seventy-five

COPY THAT

Folks who journal on a regular basis will tell you writing sets them on a path to self-discovery. So let's incorporate an exercise for writing. Let's compose a letter to ourselves that we will read in five, ten, or twenty years. (Do all three if you feel inclined.)

- When did pain start to interfere with life as I once knew it?
- What things do I value about self?
- How has having chronic pain changed my viewpoint?
- What new things have I learned about me because of pain?
- How has pain affected my relationships?
- What new thing did I learn that I didn't know before because of pain?
- Who am I now?
- Have I accepted what is?
- Have I turned obstacles into triumphs?
- Who do I hope to be when I read this letter again?

I will tuck this away, and update it when I want to reflect on where I am on my journey, where I have been and how far I have come.

ONE STEP FORWARD ...

❧ *W*inter ❧
Day Seventy-six

Is Your Carriage Headed the Right Direction?

... and two steps back.

Setbacks, reversals, deterioration, and lapses are part of any recovery process. It is a rare exception in which progress is the only direction.

Initially we struggle to accept, backsliding from time to time, but we maintain forward momentum, coping, defining, and defending our new life.

We may not prevent struggles, but one thing is for certain, if we don't expect they are part of a process, we will be stuck in a deafening position of defeat.

What has happened to me recently that caused me to struggle mentally, emotionally, physically, or spiritually?

How can I use it as my benchmark for one-step forward?

179

"Our lives are a sum total of the choices we have made."

~Dr. Wayne Dyer, author of
Wishes Fulfilled: Mastering the Art of Manifesting,
21 Days to Master Success and Inner Peace, and more...

❧ *Winter* ❧
Day Seventy-seven

Self, Trust, and a Legacy

Chronic pain and illness can cause us to become withdrawn, angry, or both. Initially, it's difficult to see any opportunity in adversity. However, we must work toward getting past denial, fear and anger, blame, and feelings of depression and isolation so we can gain forward momentum.

When others question our truthfulness regarding our pain, it creates feelings of distrust. They may be sitting in the seat of judgment (theirs to own, not ours), or maybe it's our perception. Either way, we must find a way to reboot our thinking. We may find the greatest power is in how we react, regardless if judgment (theirs or ours) is true or untrue, we benefit.

Every good motivational speaker will tell us to surround ourselves with successful people in order to experience personal achievement. A good way of doing this is to pick a role model, someone we admire for how he or she has dealt a spinal cord injury, cancer, or a chronic illness. (Mine are Christopher and Dana Reeve). Role models teach us how to create our own legacy. We learn new ways of coping by following a mentor who has had success in dealing with catastrophic illness. It gives us the strength and empowerment we need and can share.

A role model can be anyone who is well thought of for fighting his or her fight.

I will make a list of people to consider as my role model, my mentor.

I will look for the things they do that made me consider them as someone I respect.

I will find self, trust, and my own legacy.

Notes

ॐ

Some days it's difficult to find the beauty,
but I am always comforted by knowing it is ever present.

~ Celeste

❧ *W*inter ❧
Day Seventy-eight

Traffic Jam

Pain and fatigue can cause agitation, emotional stress, irritation, restlessness, and the inability to interact with others appropriately. Disordered thought processes, ineffective support structures, and poor time management further complicate this pool of symptoms. How can we avoid a traffic jam?

- Identify times of the day when our pain is most difficult.
- Assess the effect of sleep quality and quantity on our pain.
- Assess the adequacy of available support.
- Assess treatment success and failure.
- Yield to the warning signs don't force beyond limits.
- Change our perceptions to minimize tragic thinking.
- Demand to be treated with dignity and respect.

Knowing the elements of a traffic jam helps us avoid being stuck in a bumper-to-bumper situation.

Which one of these is most likely to create a traffic jam for me?

*"Oh, my friend,
it's not what they take away from you that counts.
It's what you do with what you have left."*

~Hubert Humphrey, 1911 – 1978

❧ *W*inter ❧
Day Seventy-nine

Brain Power – Exercising the Mind

Michael Michalko has written a brilliant book, *Creative Thinkering: Putting Your Imagination to Work,* Michael says, "You cannot will a new idea."

He says it is about changing our thinking patterns. In this particular case, he says, "Suppose you want to improve the flashlight. If you compare it to other flashlights, you are thinking inside the box. Instead, conceptually blend your thinking patterns by comparing a flashlight to a garage door opener."

I thought about this and the way our brain is wired when it comes to conceptualizing pain. Maybe, when we try to tell our brain to think differently comparing our pain to the branches of a tree for instance, we can see infinite possibilities. When we compare contrasts and similarities, it changes the way we think about it.

What gray matter aerobics can I perform to exercise my mind today, and how can I think outside the box when it comes to comparing my experiences with pain?

187

"There are two primary choices in life:
to accept conditions as they exist, or
accept the responsibility for changing them."

--Dr. Denis Waitley, author of
The Psychology of Winning,
Wordmaster: Improve Your Word Power, and more...

❧ *W*inter ❧
Day Eighty

Custom Fit!

Valuable treatments are ones that fit our personality and our individual needs. If it feels right, do it! We are more likely to stick to it and will be rewarded with the benefits. Here are a few you might check out.

- Acupressure
- Acupuncture
- Active Release Therapy (ART)
- Biofeedback
- Craniosacral therapy
- Hellerwork
- Massage therapy
- Myofascial release
- Reflexology
- Rosen method
- Tennis ball self-treatment
- Theracane self-treatment
- Trager work
- Trigger point massage therapy

How can I customize my interventions to fit my personality and my physical needs?

"You can make more friends in two months by becoming interested in other people than you can in two years by trying to get other people interested in you."

~Dale Carnegie

❧ *Winter* ❧
Day Eighty-one

Admiration

After learning their name, Dale Carnegie always asked for a person's birthday. He made a note and added it to his master list in his office. That person got a birthday card from Carnegie for life. He believed that the best way to get things done was to help others want to do what you want to do. A small kindness, a birthday remembered, might make all the difference.

What qualities do people you admire possess? If you could observe those people for a day what do you think you would see. What struggles do they experience? How would they deal with a roadblock? What admirable qualities do you share with them? What is the simplest way to amplify those qualities in you?

> When's your birthday?
>
> What qualities do you admire in others?

What is it I like about my favorite people?

I will reserve my energy for those who ask the question
and wait for the answer.

~ Celeste

✒ *Winter* ✒
Day Eighty-two

Thriving Midst the Thorn Bushes

Sometimes we let people make us feel we are to blame for our pain, as if we did something wrong. We have met them; we know them as "judgers." If only we had lived better, we would not have pain; if only we had tried this or tried that, we wouldn't be sick; if only we would buck up, as they do, we could tough it out, if only…

> "The one judged may sometimes be guilty as charged, but usually not. The key point is that the one judging is also guilty at some time. Thus the projection that the other (sick one) is slacking (I did), and umbrage and emotional escalation follow. Correct response to the judgment? "Don't we all, sometimes, give less than 100 percent?"
>
> (Excerpt from *Integrative Therapies for Fibromyalgia, Chronic Fatigue Syndrome, and Myofascial Pain*… See the final pages for more information)

We shouldn't let others make us feel guilty or weak because we have a painful disorder. Those of us who have pain everyday are survivors. We all have self-appointed keepers, but only we can hold them in a position of judge and jury.

Only I can let others put me on the defensive.
Repeat–Repeat–Repeat

 193

If you find a good doctor, stick with him
'till one of you die.

~Jeff

❧ *Winter* ❧
Day Eighty-three

Tips for Finding the Right Doctor

Learning how to express our feelings, focus on positives, and communicate needs is helpful, but finding the right doctor is just as important.

Here are some tips:

- Get referrals from local agencies, i.e. Arthritis Foundation or pain advocacy groups.
- Network within a support group.
- Check physician credentials with their specialty board.
- Keep in mind the doctor's age in reference to your own.
- Ask questions, such as how long it takes to get appointment?"
- Think about office location and ease of access.
- Are doctor's office hours compatible with your needs?
- The right doctor :
  - o Listens.
  - o Treats you with respect.
  - o Explains things so that you understand them without becoming impatient.
- How does the office staff treat you?

What tips did I find helpful for my own quest in finding the right doctor?

When I allow time for pain, I create time for healing;
understanding I cannot have one without
the other, keeps me in check.

~ Celeste

❧ *Winter* ❧
Day Eighty-four

Word Dirt and the Magnifying Glass
Terms to Describe Your Symptoms

aching, agitated, anxious, blistering, blotchy, bruised, burning, ceaseless, chilling, churning, clenching, cold, comes and goes, confused, constant, cramping, creepy, crippling, deep, depressed, diffuse, digging, disabling, discolored, dizzy, dry, dull, electric, exhausted, extreme, feathery, feverish, fluctuating, flushed, fluttering, forgetful, frequent, on fire, flu like, gnarling, gradual, grinding, gripping, heavy, incessant, inflamed, immobilizing, intense, intermittent, irritable, itchy, jarring, jittery, in knots, lax, light-headed, localized, nagging, nauseating, needles, nervous, numb, one-sided, painful, palpitating, patchy, piercing, penetrating, persistent, pins, poking, positional, pounding, prickly, progressive, pulling, pulsating, radiating, raw, recurring, referred, restless, rigid, ringing, scattered, scalding, searing, sensitive, sharp, shooting, slurred, sore, spasm, stiff, stinging, stuffy, stumbling, sudden, superficial, swollen, taut, tender, tense, throbbing, unusual tick, tingling, tired, tormenting, twisting, twitching, unbearable, unequal, unrelenting, unstable, vice like, vomiting, waxing and waning, wasting, weak, wormy, widespread, woozy.

What words can I use to describe my symptoms to my healthcare provider more effectively?

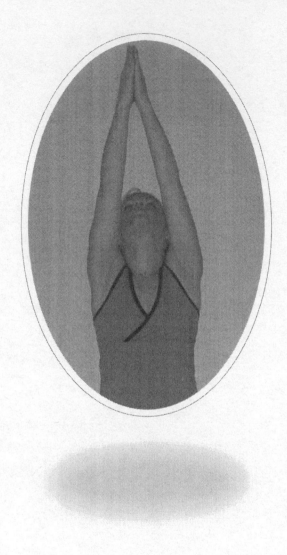

"The process of respiration is very simple.
When you breathe, you inspire.
When you don't, you expire."

~Swami Beyondananda (Steve Bhaerman), author of
When You See a Sacred Cow, Milk It for All It's Worth,
Driving Your Own Karma, and more...

❧ *Winter* ❧
Day Eighty-five

chi = qi = prana = air

Traditional Chinese Medicine (TCM) uses the term chi, or qi for what they believe is the vital life energy. Japanese medicine calls it "qi." In Ayurvedic medicine, it is known as "prana," and gong means work or "practice."

Qi Gong translates to "air work."

Good breathing has many glorious benefits to health, happiness, and feelings of well-being. The value of correctly executed deep breathing and practice, such as Qi Gong has been well documented.

We know that stress causes a rise in blood pressure, heart rate, and even temperature. We also know that oxygen is needed for cellular metabolism and when oxygen is deprived, cellular damage occurs. Oxygen is the healing life force. This is why a controlled meditative breathing practice like Qi Gong can be beneficial.

Proper breathing technique is explained on *Day Seventy-three*, **To Inspire or to Expire**, of the *Fall Devotions* book in this series. (Found at www.amazon.com/dp/B009OQJB8I)

I will direct the healing energy of Qi to areas of pain.

*The power of physical, emotional, mental, and spiritual
balance creates mindfulness. Whether in sorrow or joy,
in pain or triumph, I strive for this awareness
for others and myself.*

~ Celeste

❧ *Winter* ❧
Day Eighty-six

Stress Journaling – Sassy Talk

We have, and will, discuss different types of journaling throughout this book series, and one we should consider is keeping a journal regarding the things that stress us out. If we haven't done it, maybe we should. After all, if we don't know what creates stress in us, how can we develop tools to manage tension and pressure when it makes its way into our lives? Living with chronic pain puts us at greater risk for becoming stressed out, so let's do something about it.

Questions to ask when confronted with a stressful situation:

- Is the event something I deal with regularly?
- Do I react before having all the facts?
- Do I let stress overwhelm me?
- Do my reactions fit the crime?
- What has worked in the past?
- What can I learn from this?

I will put these questions in my journal to refer to when experiencing a stressful situation.

I have found my stride by keeping time to
a different drummer, so I dance.

~ Celeste

❧ *Winter* ❧
Day Eighty-seven

Body Chatter

Our body does believe everything we have to say about it, and changing our dialogue is important to make sure that body chatter is as positive as we can make it, even when things seem difficult to bear.

Our inner dialogue can be cluttered with limiting words and thoughts like "can't," "impossible," "not for me," and "if only." Correcting these ideas and replacing them with sensible optimistic thoughts allows experimentation, sustained effort, and new possibilities. Some of my best lessons came from doing physical therapy in a hospital and observing the defeatist attitudes that hobbled some of my fellow patients. I told my physical therapist that day that I was committed to walking out of that hospital on my own legs and I did.

Don't surrender before you get out of bed; instead listen to your body chatter and learn how to speak back. (See *Day Sixty-six.*)

My body says to me...

I say to my body...

"There are only two ways to live your life.
One is as though nothing is a miracle.
The other is as if everything is."

~Albert Einstein

*~ W*inter *~*

Day Eighty-eight

When I ...

by Celeste Cooper

> When I walk my path with purpose,
> I acknowledge the presence of challenge.
> It is when I embrace it,
> I capture the offering.
>
> When I smile at a frowning world,
> I make a difference,
> Because there are times when
> The world smiles at me.
>
> The challenge is mine to hold.
> Self-realization comes
> When I understand what I do with it
> Determines its worth.

How does my walk with pain create or interfere with my inner perceptions?

Where is the joy in life if you fail to laugh at yourself?
I find there are plenty of opportunities.

~ Celeste

❧ Winter ❧
Day Eighty-nine

Self Like – Like Self

Before we can like others, we need to like ourselves. When juggling chronic pain and its many sidekicks, we can sometimes lose track of our own self worth. By digging deep and exploring what it is we like about ourselves, we set the standard for liking others.

Here's an exercise. Write down some of your favorite words, and then explain what it is about yourself that makes you like these particular words.

Here's an example of some like words:

- animals
- balance
- boats
- building
- cars
- cooking
- family
- fishing
- gardening
- aromas
- birds
- books
- campfires
- children
- exploring
- friends
- flowers
- gatherings

- holidays
- joy
- leading
- listening
- movies
- nature
- people
- quiet
- reading
- snow
- sun
- tasting
- travel
- warmth
- woodworking
- hunting
- laughter
- learning
- mountains
- music
- opportunities
- picnics
- rain
- smiles
- stories
- talking
- touch
- walking
- water
- writing

Now write down your own like words or use these to describe how they trigger memories that affect you in a positive way. Explore self like while you like yourself.

Find tips for writing an "I AM" poem in the *Summer Devotions* available at www.amazon.com/dp/B00D665FPK

Find tips for writing poetry and see an example of an "I Like" poem in the *Fall Devotions* available at www.amazon.com/dp/B009OQJB8I

I like myself because …

Notes

ॐ

" A friend knows the song in my heart and
sings it to me when my memory fails."

~Donna Roberts, author of
Good Food Cookbook for Dogs and more…

❧ *W*inter ❧
Day Ninety

Heartstrings

As patients in pain, we have endured many expensive tests and procedures that don't render the results we desire. All these things we do in an effort to reclaim our lives as they were before. The cause isn't the issue; it is the effect.

Most of us have experienced a grocery load of different medication trials, some to no avail, some that have done more harm than good, and some that have helped, but the one thing most of us agree on is that we WANT to be in touch with our reality despite what that means regarding pain. We WANT to experience life, not stumble through it in a fog, whether the fog is the result of untreated pain or medications that interfere with our quality of life.

Sometimes we don't get what we want; sometimes it is better to be numb than experience severe life altering pain, but it is up to us to decide the parameters of a meaningful life. We want to be in touch with our world, our family, and our friends. It is up to us to let those around us know that we still have a song in our heart and the desire to sing.

EPILOGUE

"Healing does not mean curing; [it] implies the possibility for us to relate differently to illness...to see with eyes of wholeness...coming to terms with things as they are."

~Jon Kabat-Zinn
(Letting Everything Become Your Teacher:
100 Mindfulness Lessons.
IL: Delta Publishing Co, 2009.)

INDEX

ABOUT THE AUTHOR, Celeste Cooper, RN, BSN

ॐ

Celeste Cooper is a retired advanced trained registered nurse who has transformed the way she copes with her own chronic pain. In her previous life, which she now thinks of as "before transformation," she was an educator, paralegal advisor, and caregiver. She received daily rewards from patients and students, and she appreciated the opportunity to be paid for something she loved to do. That all changed when overwhelming pain and chronic illness entered her life. She learned to navigate the road so many share with her, and she believes surviving the roadblocks, stumbles and all, have made her a better person. She feels fortunate to be able to use her time and talents with a purpose she believes is her legacy.

She is an advocate, and she is an expert on fibromyalgia at ShareCare.com, an online health forum. She participates in the Pain Action Alliance to Implement a National Strategy, http://PAINSproject.org, which is an initiative of the Center for Practical Bioethics created to assist in the implementation of the Institute of Medicine report "Relieving Pain in

America: A Blueprint for Transforming Prevention, Care, Education, and Research."

She is lead author of the 434-page book *Integrative Therapies for Fibromyalgia, Chronic Fatigue Syndrome, and Myofascial Pain: The Mind-Body Connection* and the *Broken Body, Wounded Spirit: Balancing the See-Saw of Chronic Pain* four book series. (*See other books by Celeste Cooper and Jeff Miller.*)

Celeste is committed to helping others turn their own "road blocks" into a "road trip" full of opportunities.

> *"What is life? It is the flash of a firefly in the night. It is the breath of a buffalo in the wintertime. It is the little shadow which runs across the grass and loses itself in the sunset."*
>
> ~Crowfoot,
> Blackfoot warrior and orator

You can Read more about Celeste: on her author page at Amazon www.amazon.com/author/celestecooper, about her role as healthcare expert on Sharecare.com at www.sharecare.com/user/celeste-cooper and check out her website at www.TheseThree.com for more helpful patient information and links to her blog, social networks, and advocacy projects.

ABOUT THE AUTHOR, Jeff Miller, PhD

ॐ

Among other interests, Jeff values working with patients with chronic pain and illness. Through his expertise, he is able to help his clients cope with the many aspects of chronic illness. Jeff offers a variety of techniques including cognitive restructuring, biofeedback, hypnosis, and proactive utilization of gifts and skills from areas of strength adapted to areas of challenge.

His interest in chronic illness has become a sub-specialty, blending his pragmatic counseling with the individual's spiritual perspective. Jeff's goal for his life/work is to reduce suffering and help others live to their true potential. For him, the work is about reducing suffering and living to your fullest potential. Jeff's mantra is, *"If you want courage as your companion, do it now, do it even though you judge that courage insufficient because it is a diminishing thing, like water held in your palms. You will never be this brave again until the next time you face this. Then you will see (as you have seen) the smallest action is mightier than the noblest intention."*

Jeff is currently in his 37th year of post–graduate education, having secured the enviable position of "paid student" by sitting in his comfortable office and awaiting his hourly lessons from folks who somehow believe he is there to help them. He is grateful, above all else, for the trust of thousands of people in pain and for the nourishing unconditional love of his family. Jeff also gratefully acknowledges the guidance of many colleagues, especially his first boss who taught him which end of the horse he did not want to be.

Jeff is co–author with Celeste of *Integrative Therapies for Fibromyalgia, Chronic Fatigue Syndrome, and Myofascial Pain: The Mind-Body Connection.* Healing Arts Press: Vermont, 2010, and Broken Body, Wounded Spirit: Balancing the See-Saw of Chronic Pain [Series], ImPress Media.

Jeff's website: http://jeffmiller.org

Other books written by Celeste Cooper and Jeff Miller
(Available in worldwide markets)

Broken Body, Wounded Spirit:

Balancing the See-Saw of Chronic Pain,

FALL DEVOTIONS

ImPress Media, Revised 2014.

Amazon in paperback

www.amazon.com/dp/0615638082

Kindle version,

http://www.amazon.com/dp/B009OQJB8I

Amazon UK www.amazon.co.uk/dp/0615638082

Amazon Canada www.amazon.ca/dp/0615638082

Barnes and Nobel

www.barnesandnoble.com/w/1113582492?ean=9780615
638089

Broken Body, Wounded Spirit:
Balancing the See-Saw of Chronic Pain,
SUMMER DEVOTIONS

ImPress Media, Revised 2014.

Amazon in paperback
www.amazon.com/dp/0615798268

Kindle version
www.amazon.com/dp/B00D665FPK

Amazon UK
www.amazon.co.uk/dp/0615798268

Amazon Canada
www.amazon.ca/dp/0615798268

Barnes and Nobel
www.barnesandnoble.com/w/1115477515?ean
=9780615798264

Broken Body, Wounded Spirit:

Balancing the See-Saw of Chronic Pain,

SPRING DEVOTIONS

ImPress Media, Revised 2014.

Amazon in paperback

http://www.amazon.com/dp/0615958664/

Kindle version

http://www.amazon.com/dp/B00J1AOAR4

Amazon UK

http://www.amazon.co.uk/dp/0615958664/

Amazon Canada

http://www.amazon.ca/dp/0615958664/

Barnes and Nobel

http://www.barnesandnoble.com/w/11189345

77?ean=9780615958668

Integrative Therapies for Fibromyalgia,

Chronic Fatigue Syndrome, and Myofascial Pain:

The Mind body Connection

Vermont: Healing Arts Press, 2010

ॐ

Inner Traditions: Healing Arts Press (Publisher)

http://store.innertraditions.com/pages/browse

Amazon in paperback

www.amazon.com/dp/1594773238

Kindle version

www.amazon.com/dp/B003ZHVBAI

Amazon UK

www.amazon.co.uk/dp/1594773238

Amazon Canada.

www.amazon.ca/dp/1594773238

Barnes and Nobel

www.barnesandnoble.com/w/1112172406?ean
=9781594773235

Nook Book

www.barnesandnoble.com/w/1112172406?ean
=9781594779596

ॐ

Made in the USA
Charleston, SC
01 October 2015